METHODISM

in

RECOVERY

METHODISM

in

RECOVERY

RENEWING MISSION
RECLAIMING HISTORY
RESTORING HEALTH

William B. Lawrence

Abingdon Press
Nashville

METHODISM IN RECOVERY
RENEWING MISSION, RECLAIMING HISTORY, RESTORING HEALTH

Copyright © 2008 by Abingdon Press

All rights reserved.

This book is printed on acid-free paper.

Library of Congress Cataloging-in-Publication Data

Lawrence, William B. (William Benjamin), 1946–
  Methodism in recovery : renewing mission, reclaiming history, restoring health / William B. Lawrence.
    p. cm.
  Includes bibliographical references.
  ISBN 978-0-687-49188-9 (binding: adhesive, perfect, pbk. : alk. paper)
  1. Church renewal—United Methodist Church (U.S.) 2. Church renewal—Methodist Church. 3. United Methodist Church (U.S.) 4. Methodist Church—United States. I. Title.
  BX8382.2.L39 2008
  287'67309051—dc22

                                                                  2008000988

08 09 10 11 12 13 14 15 16 17—10 9 8 7 6 5 4 3 2 1
MANUFACTURED IN THE UNITED STATES OF AMERICA

CONTENTS

PREFACE

By most objective measurements, Methodism is a vigorous movement within the global Christian community. When the World Methodist Council meets, its participants come from 132 countries and represent seventy-five million people. That means its total number of adherents is larger than the world's Anglican Communion. Besides sheer size, it is an extraordinarily diverse body. Africans, Europeans, Latinos, North Americans, and Asians are all constituents of the global Methodist presence. Though all Methodists trace their lineage to John Wesley, there are now seventy-six denominations within the World Methodist Council. Some are churches within the boundaries of a single nation. Others, like The United Methodist Church, are global bodies in themselves. That can lead to confusion, of course, as in Nigeria where there is both a "Methodist" Church and a "United Methodist" Church. But there is no questioning the vibrancy of the movement internationally, the unity of its historic lineage tracing back to Mr. Wesley, or the diversity of its cultural and linguistic and liturgical expressions.

The infrastructure of global Methodism is impressively strong. Educational institutions, including theological academies, exist in many places in every inhabited continent. Congregations gather for worship in grand buildings and in bush clearings. Networks of volunteers deploy teams across national boundaries to build schools, health-care clinics, and homes for orphaned children, as well as houses of worship. In some places, Methodists hold positions of great privilege; the king of Tonga, for instance, also heads the Methodist Church in his realm. In other places, Methodists occupy positions of relative powerlessness; Malaysia is officially a Muslim country, and Methodists are a distinct minority of the nation. Yet there are six annual conferences serving multiple ethnic groups of Malaysians, ranging from the reasonably wealthy in areas like the nation's capital to the subsistence poor who live along the nation's rivers.

Methodism across the globe embraces a hardy, hearty, mission-driven body of people. In Singapore, which is broadly tolerant of diverse religious groups, Methodists have established strong congregations, have conducted an effective evangelistic outreach into countries including Thailand and Vietnam, and have even championed such progressive causes as the rights of gay, lesbian, and transgendered persons. In Albania, where Methodist missions launched in the nineteenth century were only minimally effective and where a religiously intolerant brand of Communist rule precluded almost any church activity during the twentieth century, Methodism reappeared in the 1990s and is now a growing presence.

And in the United States, there is an array of Methodist bodies, including but not limited to The Korean Methodist Church, The African Methodist Episcopal Church, The Christian Methodist Episcopal Church, The African Methodist Episcopal Zion Church, and The United Methodist Church.

The last of these is clearly the largest. It provides most of the financial resources for the denomination's global presence. And it offers, if anything, a stronger presence than its size would indicate. Current official statistics suggest that United Methodists make up about 3 percent of the total United States population. But United Methodists occupy 13 percent of the seats in the United States Senate and 11 percent of the seats in the House of Representatives. When George W. Bush and Dick Cheney were challenged by John Kerry and John Edwards in the 2004 presidential election, three of the four had some claim to being United Methodist.

The presence of United Methodism is pervasive. The popular Starbucks chain of coffee shops has about twelve thousand locations worldwide, United Methodists have three times that many local churches in the United States alone. By 2012, Starbucks hopes to have more than twenty-three thousand shops across the globe.[1] That will still leave it two-thirds as widespread as United Methodist congregations are today in North America. United Methodism has a local church in more than 90 percent of the counties in the country. It has ties to scores of health-care, elder-care, child-care, and other social service agencies. It also has affiliations with more than a hundred colleges and universities. Its total annual revenues from local church offerings exceed five billion dollars, making it as big a business as a Fortune 500 company. Its property holdings are immense.

In a nation where 10 percent of the gross domestic product is generated by the nonprofit sector, The United Methodist Church is a very substantial institution with a very sizable footprint.

Yet the wider image—indeed, the wider self-image—of the church presents a much gloomier picture. Customary analyses point to significant declines in membership and worship attendance during the past forty years, and even more precipitous declines in attendance at the local churches' Sunday schools—a major mechanism for nurturing and discipling members, including especially its younger membership prospects.

Even in areas where the church seems to be growing, the increases tend to lag behind the growth in regional population. When an area like north Texas experiences a population increase of 10 percent in a given period and church membership increases by less than 1 percent, then the church is actually in a state of decline—though within a particular local church on an average Sunday there will be no apparent evidence of that decline. The pews may remain packed, the parking lot may remain full, and the budget may be well funded. But those observations obscure the fact that, relative to its context, the church's presence is ebbing.

Dismay about the denomination, moreover, is based on more than numbers.

Political and ethical and social debates over a host of issues have exposed deep fault lines within the church. There are ceaseless arguments over the restrictive language in the denomination's Social Principles regarding sexual orientation and the prohibitive language in the denomination's legislation regarding the ordination of gay and lesbian persons. Denominational agencies are either unknown or untrusted—or both. Talk of schism and separation is hard to quash.

There are disagreements over what actually constitutes the core principles of the Wesleyan theological heritage. In general, United Methodists have sat rather loosely and comfortably with their doctrinal documents. American Methodists, who have not had a real heresy trial in more than a century, are more likely to sing their theological principles about salvation and the sacraments than they are to file ecclesiastical grievances against one another regarding them. Indeed, when The United Methodist Church was formed by the merger of The Evangelical United Brethren and The Methodist Church, a question was raised about the compatibility of the theological documents that had been officially and separately affirmed by the merging bodies. An appeal to Methodism's Judicial Council led to the decision that its assignment was to rule on matters of church law not on matters of church theology. So the merger was consummated and the two possibly conflicting doctrinal statements are still both published in the denomination's *Book of Discipline* as historic documents.[2]

Nevertheless, voices within United Methodism have labored and lobbied for a more precise, and more precisely enforced, body of doctrine. The Confessing Movement was formed in the 1990s for just such a purpose. Other caucuses have assembled to try fashioning alternate statements with different emphases. In some local churches of United Methodism, efforts have been launched that will require individuals to sign a doctrinal statement before receiving permission to teach Sunday school as a volunteer. Initiatives such as this give evidence that there is considerable theological fretting in the denomination.

There are also worries about the demographic profile of United Methodism. The church is aging faster than the population in general, both among its members and among its leaders. In the past twenty years, the median age of ordained elders has risen from forty-eight to fifty-two, and the percentage of elders who are age fifty-five and older has grown from 27 percent to 41 percent. Many local churches, watching their membership levels wane as the generation that took leadership after World War II passes from the scene, are finding fewer among the younger generations to take their places.

And finally there are worries about the capacity and the willingness of United Methodism to occupy a niche in the religious marketplace.

A comparison with realities of modern media may be useful. For several decades, home entertainment options available to people in the United States consisted primarily of the programming provided by three television networks. Except for a very few major cities with additional independent or nonnetwork corporate outlets, ABC, CBS, and NBC provided most of the music, the drama, the comedy, and the news that Americans could watch at home. The proliferation of superstations based in Atlanta and Chicago, the emergence of cable and satellite delivery systems, the advancements in analog and digital recording technology through tape and disk and TiVo, and the option of downloading films through the Internet to a home computer generated numerous possibilities that did not exist in the relatively recent past.

Similarly, in the middle of the twentieth century, it was still possible to speak of mainline Protestant denominations and the Roman Catholic Church as the predominant religious options in the United States. In 1950, 90 percent of Christians participated in 114 identifiable denominations, churches, and organizations. By the year 2000, in order to identify the denominations, churches, and organizations that were serving 90 percent of the American people, it was necessary to count 675 church bodies. By that measurement, the average person seeking a church option had six times as many choices in 2000 as an individual had fifty years earlier.

And that is before one counts the non-Christian religious options for Americans who reside in or who have immigrated to the United States, as well as the culturally and constitutionally acceptable personal freedom to choose no religion or anti-religion.

Generally speaking, a smaller percentage of Americans participate in worship now than in any era since the late 1930s. Perhaps the period during and for a decade or two following World War II was an aberration in the ratio of Americans who regularly practiced religious life. Perhaps it was not, as one wing of the church likes to assert, some liberal drift in the major denominations (including Methodism) that contributed to the church's decline. Perhaps it was not, as another wing of the church likes to assert, the inadequacies of evangelism that emphasize immediate emotional response at the expense of long-term formative discipleship. Perhaps, beginning in the 1960s, the nation merely returned to its normal patterns of religious practice after recovering from the anxiety and trauma of the world war. A snapshot of that behavioral pattern was visible in the fall of 2001. Worship attendance rose dramatically in the weeks immediately following September 11, 2001, but soon settled back into pre-attack patterns.

Simple explanations of what ails Methodism, such as the rise of liberal attitudes and the rejection of conservative attitudes, may be convenient diagnoses. But that does not make them correct. Perhaps such simplified explanations are simply wrong. Perhaps such attractive analyses are appealing, but misleading.

Methodism is a significant presence with a capacity to offer a powerful voice in the world. But Methodism, including especially The United Methodist Church, feels itself in the doldrums. It is more feeling than it is fact.

To call it despair, however, would be to declare the situation hopeless.

Some years ago, the leaders of one annual conference in United Methodism gathered to ponder problems with their budget. For what was then the current fiscal period and for the period in the immediate future, projected revenues and projected expenditures looked badly out of balance. Someone in the room proposed that the bishop communicate directly to the clergy and the congregations of the conference that a "crisis" existed in their financial affairs. Another person proposed that the word "crisis" was too extreme and offered the suggestion that the bishop call it a "dilemma." A third person in the room noted that "dilemma" actually is defined as a set of circumstances in which more than one alternative is available and that all of the alternatives will lead to negative outcomes; but a "crisis" is defined as an exceptional situation that presents multiple alternatives, at least one of which will lead to a positive outcome.

Perhaps Methodism, including United Methodism, is facing a crisis. If so, there is at least hope for recovery.

Toward that end, it is my hope that this book will be of some help.

In preparing it, I am mindful of the countless Methodists who have formed my life and shaped my career. My forebears were generations of laboring-class Welsh, Cornish, English, and other European families. Most of the men were coal miners, and most of the women were homemakers in houses owned by the coal companies. Both of my grandfathers worked in the darkness below ground. One of them became a self-taught electrician, rising to be the chief electrician for the coal company, which meant he had to keep the pumping stations and the ventilation systems operating around the clock for the safety and survival of the other miners. The other grandfather was one of those working miners whose safety was protected by the pumps and the air handlers and the labor union that Methodism endorsed. My father avoided the dangers and uncertainties of the mines by quitting school in the eighth grade and later apprenticing himself to a plumber, so that he could learn a marketable trade. My mother, who may have been the first of my direct forebears to finish high school, had a career as a registered nurse.

On Sundays, none of those things was central to our way of life. The Methodist Church was. The little church building in Alden

Station, Pennsylvania, was where both sets of grandparents, along with aunts and uncles and assorted cousins, took their seats in the pews near my parents and my sister and me. That was where we went to Sunday school. It was where we took part in the youth programs and Christmas pageants. And, in the years that followed, it was where the extended families gathered for funerals, including the funeral for my father in 1992.

That was also the place where a young student pastor named Doug Akers became an adviser, mentor, and friend. He encouraged me in the direction of my undergraduate education. He guided me and became an advocate for me in the process that led to my ordination. He, along with the pastor of the United Methodist church that was my wife's home congregation, shared in our wedding service in 1969. He assisted in laying hands upon me when I was ordained an elder in the church in 1972.

There have been many places and many persons along the way who have opened doors for me, opened their hearts to me, and opened their minds with me in an effort to open mine. With gratitude to all of them and with shared concern for the recovery of the church that has nurtured us, I have prepared these pages, knowing that my most profound gratitude of all on this earth goes to my wife, Naomi. A lifelong Methodist herself, she has traveled many miles with me, moved into and out of many parsonages and houses, found ways to make all of them great homes for the two of us as well as our two sons, and pondered with me what the recovery of Methodism might mean.

INTRODUCTION

"[There is] a time to be born, and a time to die."

(Ecclesiastes 3:2)

I n the summer of 2007, two tragic events occurred in the United States that galvanized the attention of the nation for many days. One involved an explosion inside a Utah coal mine. The other involved a bridge collapse in Minnesota. That the first event would ever happen is hardly a shock—coal mining has long been known as one of the most dangerous occupations in existence. That the second occurred should not have been a surprise either. As engineering professor Henry Petroski has shown, major bridge failures before the Minnesota collapse "occurred at intervals of approximately thirty years."[1] Specifically, they happened in 1847, 1879, 1907, 1940, and 1970. So a catastrophic bridge failure in the year 2000 or soon thereafter was predictable.

That such incidents could have been foreseen, however, is not the point. Everyone understands that mining is dangerous, but no one can predict with certainty which mine will collapse or when. Everyone should understand that a significant bridge failure will occur about once in each generation, but no one can predict with confidence which bridge will crumble at what time. Human beings are prescient enough to weigh the risks, but not to know in advance the realities. At best, we can prepare for the tragedies, crises, failures, and emergencies. What truly matters is our response to them.

Rescue

In the immediate aftermath of an extreme event, the first response is *rescue.* People on the scene and those who arrive in the moments immediately following the disaster do everything possible to find those who are trapped, care for those who are hurt, remove the injured from a place of further harm, and redeem them from being exposed to additional risk.

Often those efforts are instinctive; occasionally they are heroic. In the wake of the Minnesota bridge collapse, for instance, a school bus carrying children on a summer field trip was caught on the precipice of the broken span. A young man whose assignment was to chaperone the youngsters had no special training for handling such an emergency, but he followed his impulse to kick open a door and move the children to safety. There are some persons whose instincts would have been to save themselves. This young man chose to save others. As a result, all of the children in the teetering bus were rescued because he took action.

Perhaps even more often than instinctive, these efforts at rescue are the result of careful as well as thoughtful planning. Emergency medical personnel train rigorously to be ready for responding to disasters and rescuing the injured. Nevertheless, even rescue efforts that are carefully planned and diligently executed occasionally result in further tragedy. The search for the trapped Utah miners began with drilling some small holes into sections of the rocky mountain where the men had been working and where they might have sought refuge. To rescue them required knowing their location and, if possible, their condition. After multiple small holes were drilled, after microphones and cameras that were lowered through the holes failed to find any sounds or sight of the miners, a team of experienced rescuers was sent into the mine to search for them. Not only did the effort at rescue fail, it compounded the tragedy. The rescuers were themselves killed when another collapse of rock occurred.

The first response is to attempt a rescue. Its purpose is to prevent further harm. It may succeed in that effort. It may fail in that effort. Or, as in the case of the would-be rescuers who were sent into the Utah mine, it may deepen the tragedy.

Some persons who find themselves invited or drawn into the personal dilemmas of other individuals or households feel compelled to attempt a rescue. Is there a spouse or a child facing physical abuse? Then the person or persons at risk must be removed from the situation. Are there teenagers consorting with neighborhood gangs who will lead them into criminal activity, drug abuse, and violence? Then some intervention must occur to rescue young people from a life-wrecking or life-ending disaster. Are there individuals and families and groups struggling on the streets, living without homes or health care? Then the church in the community must open a clinic, a soup kitchen, a shelter. Is there a church in a steady state of declining membership, resources, and influence? Then forces may feel the need to act boldly and effect a rescue.

Yet the efforts to rescue may fail. Persons who appear to be at risk may deny that they are in danger. Rescuers' efforts, however well intentioned, may make the situation worse—raising the expectations of those who are in trouble, only to discover that the weight of the problems is too heavy, the resources required for rescue are too few, the motivation to sustain a rescue effort is too thin, the methods chosen by the rescuers are too misguided, or the criticism of the rescue technique being attempted is too strident.

And even if it succeeds, the rescue effort will have accomplished only a single achievement in preventing further harm at a particular moment in the wake of one terrible tragedy. It may take a retail approach to what is actually a wholesale problem. That does not mean rescue is wrong. William Booth, the founder of the Salvation Army, reportedly said to a critic of his organization's efforts to rescue people in crisis, "I like my way of doing something better than your way of doing nothing."

Rescue is not wrong. But it is limited.

At some point, rescue efforts cease. It may be that all of the discoverable victims of the tragedy have been found. It may be that so much time has elapsed there is no likely possibility of finding anyone else to rescue. It may be that there are certain finite realities in the situation limiting access to a mine in a mountain, restricting technology capable of detecting a living human being, or acknowledging that the remote possibility of finding trapped miners does not outweigh the tremendous danger of putting other searchers at risk of further loss.

It may be that, as happened in the city of New Orleans following Hurricane Katrina, the rescuers just decide that conducting rescues is not a priority and they simply quit. People were left on rooftops. People were abandoned in the Convention Center and in the Superdome. People were neglected in hospitals and nursing homes. People were left defenseless against acts of violence. For whatever reason, rescue attempts were halted. This fact was then, and still is, a national disgrace.

The choice to end rescue efforts in a particular situation may be arbitrary or necessary or obvious or premature or unwise or immoral. In any case, the choice is made. Then the first phase of the response, namely rescue, gives way to the second phase of the response.

Recovery

In the aftermath of a tragic event, that second phase is *recovery*. After the collapse of the bridge in Minnesota, after the children had been rescued from the school bus, after the drivers and passengers had been removed from the vehicles caught on the crumbling span, after people who had survived a plunge into the water were taken from the torrent, after the rescuers had moved every injured person to a facility for medical treatment, after lists had been compiled of the persons for whom an accounting could be given and of the persons who still were considered missing, and after the physical condition of the bridge remnants and the rushing stream were considered stable enough for workers to enter the scene, a grim task called recovery began. It involved locating many submerged vehicles, avoiding fragments of the fallen bridge, removing the bodies of persons who had died in the disaster, and clearing the path for waterway and roadway traffic to be restored.

A major stage in the recovery was marked when the remaining span of the bridge was reopened for one day of pedestrian traffic. Throngs of people walked. Some mourned the thirteen friends and family members who died. Many paused to reflect. More than a few wept. Others focused their attention on when and how the bridge would be rebuilt. Recovery is a grim and a necessary business.

Sometimes, recovery never happens.

In Utah, after the rescuers died trying to find the missing miners, and after additional holes drilled into the rock yielded neither sight nor sound of the men, the physical work of recovery ceased. Efforts to locate the bodies were abandoned. The mine was sealed. No more coal will ever again be taken from that mountain. It is now not a work site but a burial site. The dead miners' families will have to endure that imperfect form of grief known to persons whose loved ones have been declared "missing in action."

My first full-time appointment as a United Methodist minister was to serve as the pastor of two small churches on a charge in northeastern Pennsylvania. The year was 1971. Among the members of one congregation was a couple in their seventies. They had raised two sons. One was a single adult still living with them and working in a nearby factory. The other had served in World War II, flying aircraft in the Pacific. During the final months of the war, the parents had received word that their son's plane was last seen going down toward an island in the ocean. By the time I met them, twenty-six years had elapsed since they received that initial message about their missing son.

In that period—more than a quarter of a century—they had made countless efforts to acquire military records, to contact personnel from their son's unit, to scan data about any hospitalized individuals whose identities could not be ascertained. In two and a half decades, they had learned no new information. They continued to cling to the notion that their son was still missing. The mother continued to have nightmares that her son was in a prison camp somewhere, pleading for rescue.

She was aching for her own recovery. It never came. Upstairs in the family home, she regularly cleaned the missing son's bedroom and kept it just as it was the day he left. In the living room was a photo, taken of him that last time he was home on leave. Out in the garage, where he had parked it, was the 1939 automobile that he had purchased before donning a uniform. When she and her husband died, they took their last breaths never knowing more about their son than that he was missing. They never recovered. It fell to the surviving brother to clear out the bedroom, pack the pictures, and dispose of the car.

Sometimes, recovery never happens. Whether it does will depend on how the word "recovery" is understood. The term is a multivalent metaphor. There are three ways to interpret and understand recovery.

In one sense, it can mean gathering the shards and the residue of what has passed from the scene. Uncovering the ruins of Pompeii is a fascinating archaeological activity, and recovering its relics can lead to some remarkable information about an ancient civilization and a volcanic eruption. Recovering the bones of dinosaurs is important geologically, ecologically, and cosmologically in an effort to understand the nature of this planet, the process of creation, and the relatively meager bit of earth's history that has involved human beings. Recovering the remains of an Aztec temple in the vicinity of the Roman Catholic Cathedral in Mexico City is tremendously important anthropologically, historically, politically, culturally, and religiously. Each of these is a significant kind of recovery. But not one of them has as its purpose to reestablish the ancient Greco-Roman society, or to reintroduce extinct species, or to reinstitute a sacrificial cult in the Western Hemisphere. "Recovery" can involve assembling artifacts of another age, or collecting debris from a disaster, or dealing with death.⟩

In itself,⟨that kind of recovery has merit.⟩

But⟨there is nothing restorative about it.⟩

To recover may mean, in this sense, to gather the fragments of something that is finished and to ponder them for whatever value there is simply in having knowledge of them. This is important for scholars and antiquarians. This is why academics assemble materials for libraries and research projects. Important things can be learned about John Wesley by examining the original documents pertaining to his life, which include his letters, his tracts, his diaries, his journals. These items will not, on their own, restore his Methodist movement to greatness, but they can inform his ecclesiastical heirs with truth. And that is an important act of recovery.

In a second sense,⟨the term "recovery" is a metaphor for the restorative power of healing.⟩It is most commonly a medical image. Patients recover from infections, recover from heart attacks, recover from surgery, and recover from emotional or mental illnesses ranging from clinical depression to psychotic breakdowns.

As a metaphor, it extends well beyond the practice of medicine. Analysts try to diagnose what is happening in a business or a church and then recommend steps that might be taken for the institution to recover. The Marshall Plan helped Europe recover from World War II. Diagnostic engineering helped the Space Shuttle program at NASA recover from the disastrous explosion of *Challenger*. Agricultural assessments by some agronomists from the Carter Center diagnosed problems with plowing and planting techniques in some African countries, helping them recover from famine and turning them from food-importing nations to food-exporting nations. An accurate diagnosis and a wise treatment plan can lead to medical, political, cultural, or economic recovery.

When Thomas Watson found in the 1930s that his fledgling company called IBM was struggling to stay afloat, he was advised that his company was unhealthy because he had too many employees and he needed to dismiss some. Watson disagreed with the diagnosis, judging (against the counsel of his corporate diagnosticians) that he did not have too many employees but rather that he had too few customers. He hired more people and sent them on the road in search of more clients who might buy or lease his products. In retrospect, he was clearly correct. To assure recovery, the diagnosis must be right.

The concept of recovery has social significance. Communities recover from natural disasters like hurricanes, fires, and floods. Economies recover from recession, depression, inflation, and wartime scarcity. Businesses recover from bad corporate decisions (consider New Coke and the Edsel). Churches recover from schisms (Roman Catholicism and Orthodoxy have thrived in separation for a thousand years; Lutherans, Anglicans, and Roman Catholics endure, ecumenically divided, after half a millennium). Some politicians recover their loss of stature. Richard Nixon did it at least four times: once during his vice presidency when accusations of scandal led to his famous speech in which he spoke of his family's devotion to their dog Checkers, once after his defeat in the 1960 presidential election, once after his failed campaign to be governor of California, and a final recovery elevated him to the status of a senior statesman in the years following the unprecedented humiliation of his having to resign the presidency.

But, in this sense of recovery, there is nothing truly renewing about it. Medically, a man may fully recover from surgery for prostate cancer, but he will forever have to be vigilant about regular testing to check on the possible recurrence of the disease. In the same way, a woman may have five healthy, disease-free years following treatment for breast cancer, but she will never have an entirely new body that guarantees protection against the reappearance of malignant cells.

Recovery, as a medical metaphor, does not mean renewal. To recover from a heart attack is to live within the limits that cardiac care allows. To recover from an emotional illness is to continue indefinitely with talk therapy or pharmacological therapy or both. To recover from a political setback does not, despite aggressive public relations efforts, create a "new Nixon." To recover from a flood does not give people new lives free from the horrible memories of what was lost when the waters rose.

In the secular world of business, recovery does not mean renewal. A company may indeed be restored to profitability after disastrously bad decisions. But corporations will never recoup whatever was lost in the aftermath of terrible choices and will never be immune from equally bad—or worse—judgments in the future.

In the religious realm, recovery does not necessarily mean renewal. Everything depends on the standards that are used to assess recovery.

Churches that have divided in the distant or recent past can claim that they are alive and thriving in their separated status by exhibiting some statistical or financial success. But a positive balance sheet, a handsome property, and an impressive set of numbers documenting attendance growth do not mean that an institutional gathering of people constitutes a church. Such material marks do not make them "churches" at all. Joel Osteen leads a Houston-based ministry with worship services broadcast across the nation. He has taken the ministry well beyond what his father had achieved in an earlier, clearly successful, religious initiative. The renovation of a former basketball arena to house the operation required nearly a hundred million dollars, and the annual budget to run the operation requires half that amount in revenue. Crowds pack the arena to hear him speak. Viewers follow his programs on television. If the bad reputation engendered by some formerly famous yet deeply flawed religious celebrities like Jim Bakker and Jimmy Swaggart seemed to endanger any would-be entrepreneurial religious, Joel Osteen's achievements are an impressive sign of recovery. There is no question his venture is a success.

But is it a church?

In this second sense, recovery can mean surviving and—on some level—even thriving. It can mean regaining the signs of success after a crisis. But it will not involve transcending the crisis, for the crisis will leave its mark. Certain limitations will remain. Certain losses will not be overcome. Certain differences will be irreconcilable. Certain wounds will always be tender.

American Methodism offers a case in point.

Separation of black and white persons was the norm for most of Methodism's first three centuries. Most of the church's institutions—conferences, congregations, colleges, and campgrounds—were racially segregated. Francis Asbury, the white bishop who led and dominated the church throughout its earliest decades, often traveled (particularly in the South) with Harry Hosier, the black preacher who was widely regarded as the finest witness of the gospel in his day. But Hosier and Asbury regularly spoke to segregated audiences and slept in segregated circumstances (Asbury in the host's house; Hosier in the host's barn).

In Methodist church buildings, black worshipers were typically restricted to balconies. Yet if seats were needed for white worshipers—as happened in Philadelphia's St. George's Church in 1796—blacks would be instructed to surrender their balcony spaces. It was just such an action that led to the departure of Richard Allen and others who formed the African Methodist Episcopal Church.

The denomination's organizational systems were racially divided. In the second half of the nineteenth century, following the Civil War, black Methodists in the South found their membership shifted to a separate denomination, the Colored Methodist Episcopal Church. And, in 1939, when southern and northern Methodists reunited nearly a century following a schism in 1844 over slavery, a new entity was created within the church's organization. Five regional jurisdictions and one "Central" Jurisdiction were established, with the Central Jurisdiction embracing all of the black congregations and judicatories, regardless of their geographic region.

Late in the history of desegregation, but eventually nevertheless, the church took steps to end this racial division. In 1968, with the formation of The United Methodist Church, all churches and judicatories were grouped into regional jurisdictions, and the Central Jurisdiction was abolished. In the 1950s and 1960s, Methodist-related colleges, universities, and other institutions began to integrate. Viewed from one angle, Methodism moved beyond the system of racial segregation that was so manifest in the history of the connection.

But the church has never recovered from racist roots and systems. With a small number of notable exceptions, United Methodism's local churches today remain racially homogeneous if not racially exclusive. The political process for choosing church leaders, including bishops, remains racially charged. Legislative procedures, nominating policies, and monitoring practices have all been instituted to create diversity because inclusiveness is not yet inherent in the denomination. Caucus groups, fashioned along racial or racial-ethnic lines, are deemed essential for blacks and other ethnic minorities to have a viable voice in a church that is more than 90 percent white. From the officially recognized Black Methodists for Church Renewal to the informal caucus of "Ebony Bishops" within the Council of Bishops, the church has been populated with advocacy groups. The clear perception that such bodies are needed within the church's life is just another item of strong evidence that American Methodism is not yet fully recovered from its racism.

Of course, in the early years of the twenty-first century, race and ethnicity are not the only identifiable signs of division in the denomination. Debates over denominational doctrine, biblical interpretation, and ecclesiastical discipline are intense. Some of those differences are manifest in the heated conversations about homosexuality and abortion. All of this could lead the institution to implode organizationally. Some might argue that, operationally, it already has. That is a possibility worth examining in greater depth. Perhaps United Methodism has already, functionally, divided. Perhaps it will dissolve, even disappear.

If so, then some future writer may recover the shards of its demise, assemble its artifacts, and knowledgeably describe its death. That would be one kind of recovery of Methodism.

Or perhaps some way can be found to achieve a recovery of Methodism that involves a kind of healing. More open and honest discussion about our racist heritage, our doctrinal disputes, and our disciplinary differences could help. To the extent that the recovery of Methodism is built upon a medical metaphor, a straightforward and clear diagnosis of what ails the church seems essential. But that much candor may expose too many scars. There may be too many competing advocates for too many forms of therapy, leaving the church unable to discern what to do. Depending on who makes the diagnosis, it could be entirely wrong.

Besides, a medicalization of Methodism that pays too much attention to some supposed vital signs will miss the point. Is a decline in numbers of membership the best measurement of a church's loss of its mission? Would a growth in worship attendance be solid evidence that Methodism is in recovery? Would recovery to the membership numbers that the denomination boasted in 1968 be a sign of health? Or might such a development pay attention to a misleading statistic that cannot measure mission, passion, renewal, or effectiveness?

If a church merely recovers to the level of limited vitality, it will hardly be a face or a force or a voice to announce Christ's lordship or God's reign. Such a recovery of Methodism might be real but still be irrelevant.

There is, however, a third sense in which the term "recovery" can be understood. The first kind merely gathers together the remnants of death, grief, and loss. The second settles for a scarred, wounded, limited existence of function and operation that promotes neither passion nor potency, neither vitality nor renewal. The third kind of recovery is one that is unafraid to own its past or to claim its future. But it requires more than simply stirring the remnants of the past and more than exposing the sore spots and tender places that limit the capacity as well as the courage to live faithfully. In fact, it must transcend any medicalization of the church and embrace the mystery of the faith.

This book is a plea for that kind of recovery of Methodism. In part, it requires a recovery of what it means to be a church.

One classic way to define what constitutes a church is by two criteria—that the Word is faithfully preached and the sacraments are duly administered. Another definition adds a third criterion—that the community adheres to a proper order and discipline. Some in Methodist circles might quibble whether Methodists prefer a definition of church that includes only the first two or all three of these criteria, though it is clear that Methodism's historic emphasis on discipline means that three criteria define what constitutes church in the Methodist tradition. Meanwhile, there is no doubt that essential to the reality of the church is the unity of the church. The New Testament proclaims it: "There is one body and one Spirit . . . one Lord, one faith, one baptism" (Ephesians 4:4-5).

The recovery of Methodism, therefore, involves a renewal of unity and a renewal of three criteria for defining what constitutes church. Or, no matter what happens to its statistics of membership and revenue and property and influence, it is not recovery at all. It would be hypocritical, at best, to read a text that affirms our having one Lord, one faith, one baptism, and not measure ecclesiastical identity by those bedrock, creedal commitments.

To recover as an ecclesiastical institution is not the same as organizational success or physical endurance or fiscal survival. It must involve renewal. Somewhere in the calculation, a church's adherence to the Christian mission must be assessed, the fractures in church unity must be addressed, and institutional recovery that settles for less than renewal must remain suspect.

It matters whether ecumenical attempts at reconciliation achieve more than minimal results. It matters whether solitary attempts by separated bodies to say to the world that theirs is the only true way insist on having universal sway. It matters that other religious traditions are now our neighbors. Interfaith conversations—between Christians and Muslims, or among Pentecostal Christians and Methodist Christians and Muslims and Buddhists—are exceedingly difficult when intra-faith conversations among Christian groups are still scarred by previous battles. The recovery of the church is not merely a matter of institutional, organizational, operational endurance. It means readiness to serve in the coming age.

United Methodists in particular have been living for decades with the notion that there is a pathological problem in the denomination—a disease—whose symptoms include declining membership, declining worship attendance, declining Sunday school attendance, deteriorating stewardship, and a decaying infrastructure. But, if those are the symptoms, what is the diagnosis? Or is this merely an attempt to medicalize the church rather than to hold the movement theologically accountable? United Methodists are also suffering from a debilitating loss of hearing (an inability to listen to one another) and a debilitating loss of vision (an inability to recognize one another's differences or needs for fashioning the future of the church). Is this a medical problem needing healing, or is it a theological problem that compels the church to seek a different form of recovery?

The recovery of Methodism is not the same as an institutional reclamation of United Methodism. Whether The United Methodist Church can or should endure as an intact organization is an open question, worthy of serious consideration. The recovery of Methodism is a larger theological challenge.

Methodism does not need rescue. It does need recovery. But neither the kind of recovery that simply reassembles the artifacts of its past, nor the kind of recovery that merely marks a statistical turnaround or organizational durability will do. The recovery of Methodism requires renewal. And that will require a recovery of what it means to be the church. How does one define what constitutes a church? How do we know whether an ecclesiastical body that has gone through a crisis has reached a point of recovery? How do we know whether its recovery has restored it and renewed it to become, again, a church?

As institutions go, The United Methodist Church is relatively young. But it is seriously ailing and there are doubts about whether it will survive much longer.

Founded in 1968 by the merger of The Evangelical United Brethren and The Methodist Church, the denomination would barely be considered middle-aged if it were a person and not an organization. Should an individual man or woman face a crisis of survival at the same age, there would be many words of sorrow about dying too early. But when organizations rise and fall, they tend to evoke different sentiments. Businesses are founded and fail all the time. Yet neighbors rarely comment that the sandwich shop on the corner died too soon, if it closed after scarcely two years (let alone forty years) of struggling to survive.

The landscape is littered with big corporations that have collapsed. Airlines and Automobile makers could start the list, and one need not even reach the second letter of the alphabet to make the point. Pan Am endures as a historic name in air travel, but it no longer has a waiting list of commercial travelers who want to fly to the moon, as its advertising once boasted. Pan Am was essentially grounded after six decades of flying as the principal international carrier based in the United States. Some passengers may have regretted that, but did anybody lament that it died too young? General Motors, a gigantic corporation among the giants, was founded in 1908, and it has enjoyed roughly a century of success. But its survival as a corporation is hardly assured, and there are many who are worried about its prospects for a second century. The company may not remain intact as an organization. The Ford Motor Company bears the name of the single most significant figure in the auto industry, more important for his development of the system to build cars than for the cars that his system built. But Ford is a weakened company. How long will it survive?

How might the bereaved behave if a corporate centenarian dies? Will it have died too soon? Will it have ended after a long and happy life? Or will it be construed as a failure?

And what might one say about a church? If United Methodism is indeed on the verge of passing away, is anyone grieving that it is dying too soon?

Perhaps the questions are premature. Broken bodies mend. Depressed minds heal. Storm-tossed cities rebuild. Troubled institutions recover. Churches experience renewal. And the differences that distinguish demise from deliverance are great mysteries. So regardless of the severity of what ails The United Methodist Church, it is not yet clear whether the prospects for the future of the denomination are bright or grim. What is clear is that United Methodism's current situation requires both a confrontation with the facts and an encounter with the Spirit. Then, if it becomes necessary to conduct a wake for the organization, there will be spiritual resources for doing so. And if it happens that the organization endures, there will be spiritual resources to sustain its renewal.

This book is one United Methodist's effort to confront the facts and to invoke the Spirit. It will explore the multiple meanings of recovery and the denomination's prospect for recovering from this current crisis.

Within its chapters and pages, I will identify a number of themes that are essential to the recovery of Methodism. They will include the following:

- Learning again how to define what "church" is
- Facing the need to offer confession
- Finding better ways to make decisions
- Seeing negative circumstances as positive opportunities
- Offering a distinctive voice in the public arena
- Placing congregations in the context of connectional mission
- Connecting with all social classes, including the poor and the rich
- Changing the paradigm for debate from the political to the doctrinal
- Changing the practices of discussion from the legislative to the theological
- Forming a financial system beyond apportionment limits
- Listening to one another more than talking to ourselves

- Opening our spirituality to the power of silence
- Restoring the role of oversight to the episcopacy
- Renewing the place of Christian conferencing
- Making the mysteries of faith more accessible
- Linking hope with vision

This book will also attempt to take seriously the possibility that *the recovery of Methodism* may not require—or include—the survival of The United Methodist Church. That is part of the mystery.

CHAPTER ONE

Checking the Vital Signs

*"You hypocrites! . . . Why do you not know how to
interpret the present time?"*
(Luke 12:56)

n the early summer of 2006, I sat with about fifteen other United
Methodists in a windowless room tucked inside a Nashville office building. We were a rather random (not to say "representative") bunch—a few bishops, a few academics, and some staff
professionals from several general agencies of the denomination.
What we had in common was that all of us, in our differing types of
work, engaged in research. The topic on the agenda was to share
those facets of our research that might shed light on The United
Methodist Church. What data could our conferences, agencies, and
educational institutions provide to develop an accurate picture of the
church's present and an accurate prognosis of the church's future?

It was an inauspicious time to hold such a discussion. Most of
the annual conferences in the five regional jurisdictions within the
United States had recently concluded their 2006 sessions, and
the hard data reported at those gatherings were quite disturbing.
The denomination had continued its statistical declines in membership, worship attendance, and church school participation.

Specifically, membership had apparently fallen below eight million, in a continuing erosion of members that had begun four decades earlier.

What's more, the detailed numbers within those aggregate statistics were even more troubling. By the first decade of the twenty-first century, the decline of the denomination was unmistakably occurring even in regions of the country that had previously shown growth in the numbers of both members and attendees. While the denomination as a whole has been shrinking since its formation in 1968, at least some signs of increase had been occurring in the southern states. But the evidence compiled in 2006 brushed aside that boast as well. The Florida Conference reported a membership decline greater than 1 percent and a worship attendance decrease approaching 3 percent. The North Alabama Conference reported even larger declines in membership and worship attendance. The Texas Conference dropped more than 2 percent in membership and, though its decrease in worship attendance was smaller, there was a decrease nevertheless. The North Texas Conference experienced only a small decline in its membership, but the worship attendance figures dropped 2 percent.

So the mood in that windowless Nashville room was not sober, it was sour. Some observers had been warning for years that even where United Methodism seemed to be growing—in Florida, the Carolinas, Georgia, and Texas—the increases were only in absolute numbers. Compared with the growth in the population of these states, United Methodists have actually been decreasing proportionately. That detail may have been too subtle for some to notice, too counterintuitive for some to embrace, or too unpleasant for some to acknowledge. But facts in the statistical reports offered no refuge from reality. By the time the numbers were tallied in 2006, subtlety had subsided and intuition could not ignore the truth. The declines were evident in both absolute and relative terms.

Moreover, the group gathered in Nashville did not have to focus solely on membership and attendance. One of the bishops offered another reason to be troubled. It was financial pressure. "We can calculate the unfunded liability of our pension program," the bishop said, "and we can calculate the unfunded liability of our health insurance obligations, but we cannot calculate the unfunded liability of the guaranteed appointment." This was a reference, of course, to legislation affirmed by the General Conference and embedded in *The Book of Discipline* assuring every ordained elder that she or he will receive an appointment to some place of ministry and will receive compensation no less than the amount the annual conference sets as a minimum. What happens when declining members, reduced revenues, increased health insurance costs, expanding pension obligations, and guaranteed salaries combine to create an untenable financial situation?

It was in this heavy atmosphere that one of the academics posed a question to one of the professional agency staff. "How many years have we got? . . . In what year, given these data, do you estimate that The United Methodist Church as we know it will cease to be?"

After a long pause, the agency officer gave an answer: "2010."

His courage was admirable. His willingness to offer a direct answer instead of some bureaucratic fudge was commendable. And at least it will not take long to learn whether he was right. But the key to the question—and to his answer—was the institutional nature of it. The rescue of an ecclesiastical organization is never a priority for Christian mission. The fear of organizational failure is never an ultimate threat to the Christian mission. "The church is of God, and will be preserved to the end of time, for the conduct of worship and the due administration of God's Word and Sacraments, the maintenance of Christian fellowship and discipline, the edification of believers, and the conversion of the world." Does it really matter if The United Methodist Church endures? Or is the far more vital issue the mission of the church? And is there some possibility that the recovery of Methodism is still relevant to that mission?

To answer that question, one requires a fundamental appreciation for the fact that there is no way to rescue any institution from its own capacity to fail. In theological terms, the church has taught this as the doctrine of original sin. It does not derive from some mythic incident in a prehistoric garden that was biologically transmitted to an endless chain of human offspring. Rather, the doctrine of original sin expresses the irrepressible capacity of human pride. Martin Luther conceived of it in terms of a spiral, imagining that the human soul is curved inward upon itself. But one can find it even in recent entertainment circles. For instance, a character in the computer-animated film *The Incredibles* says, "No matter how many times you save the world, it always manages to get back in jeopardy again."

Failure is intrinsic to human life and to whatever human beings create. Often that is the case simply because our creations are so complex. When Microsoft designed its Windows 2000 operating system, it was written with twenty million lines of source code. There is no human possibility of testing for every conceivable form of error in that much mathematical text. Then Microsoft issued Windows XP, which was designed with forty million lines of source code.[2] The numbers for its next system, Vista, are surely even more staggering. Yet human activities depend upon machines and systems that are sure to have faults and to fail, because there are no flawless or faultless or fail-proof systems.

The church was established by God. But its organizational systems, its decisions about how and whom to ordain, its methods for managing financial resources, its choices about where to establish new congregations, its compromises about what will constitute authentic worship, and its willingness to show courage in fashioning new forms for fulfilling the Christian mission are imperfect.

The curious thing is that everyone in the church knows this, recognizes this, and (at least on a theoretical level) acknowledges this. And yet there is, within the church, a widespread resistance to confessing it.

I have opportunities to visit a significant number of local churches and to participate, as a worshiper or a guest speaker, in Sunday services. Many of these congregations are among the celebrated large-membership churches in United Methodism, where the Sunday attendance is calculated in the thousands. These are the congregations generally blessed with an amazing array of gifted laity and clergy who lead the ministries of the church.

Almost invariably, their Sunday worship offers magnificent music, whether it is in the more classical genre from European and North American cultures, or from some emerging Latin, Asian, Native American, or African cultures, or from the array of so-called "contemporary Christian" music styles. The preaching is typically of very high quality, the prayers have spiritual integrity and sometimes poetic elegance. In short, these are the churches that offer the most outstanding experiences of worship available.

But one thing is frequently absent from the elements of worship in these churches. Whether the liturgy is formal, with a printed program and written prayers, or informal, with a casual bulletin of announcements and spontaneous prayers, I often have noticed something missing. I have realized at the end of worship that there was no prayer of confession, no acknowledgment of sin, no declaration of forgiveness, no act of reconciliation.

There are many plausible reasons for this.

Sometimes these churches, especially the very large ones, have multiple services with crowds moving into and out of their buildings on a relatively tight schedule. Worship and other activities have to be rather closely timed. Some may be broadcast on radio or be recorded for telecast or for distribution by digital recording on the church's Web site. They may be structured to last for a preprogrammed period of fifty-five minutes. With the commitment already made to a large music budget, with a congregational expectation that a decent sermon should last some reasonable amount of time, with necessary room for programmatic announcements, and with appropriate portions of worship to enable congregational participation such as singing hymns, some things have to be eliminated. Among the options not available for exclusion are the financial offering, the words of greeting or welcome, and the choral anthems. Among the options that may be available for exclusion are the recitation of a creed, the reading or responsive chanting of a psalm, the full liturgies for administering sacraments, and prayerful practice of remaining seated in silence for the opening and closing organ voluntaries.

A relatively easy option is to eliminate the act of confession. To forgo admitting sins and announcing God's merciful gift of forgiveness and reconciliation can save two minutes or more. Thus, one reason for removing penitential words or actions from the liturgy is to increase efficiency in the use of time.

Another possible reason rests with the very fact that these churches are indeed so successful. Marvelous worship experiences, vibrant youth ministries, solid educational programming, broad community service activities, effective evangelistic outreach, and international forms of emphasis characterize their achievements in Christian mission. Moreover, the persons who tend to worship in these settings are themselves likely to be accomplished in their careers, dedicated to their spiritual development, and willing to volunteer in various ways toward the congregation's vital ministries. Confession is not always congenial to such personal and communal accomplishment.

A third possible reason is that to confess sins, as an individual or communal act, requires some level of intimacy. Of course, intimacy with God is an aspect of that. But so is a sense of intimacy, or at least comfort, with those in whose presence one is offering a penitential word. Thousands, or even hundreds, of people assembled in one place can create an impressive crowd for a shared religious experience. Having that many people sing together or shout praises together can be spiritually energizing. But how, in that context, does one find the level of intimacy needed to acknowledge a harmful deed, a racist word, an adulterous thought, a felonious act, an addictive trait, a violent temper, an abusive slap, or a crisis of faith?

Not many Christians in recent memory are viewed with an aura of saintliness quite so universally as the late Mother Teresa. Her public work was exceptional. Her public voice was powerful. Her public witness was the kind that moved many ordinary believers to new levels of compassion, devotion, and care for others. Yet only after her death has the world begun to learn about what she could not acknowledge in public—her long, dark night of the soul that endured for half a century, her sense of an "absent" Christ. Of Jesus, she wrote, "The silence and the emptiness are so great that I look and do not see, listen and do not hear."[3]

To confess what would appear to be spiritual weakness or moral failure requires an environment of comfortable intimacy with God and with the community in which the confession will occur. The quiet, private space of a confessional booth offers one such place. The intimacy and trust of a relationship with a spiritual director, pastoral counselor, monastic community, or covenant discipleship group may offer another. But a vast public space or a gathering of thousands will not be conducive to the comfortable intimacy that encourages confession.

Nor, oddly enough, will reducing the size of the crowd achieve that goal.

It is not only the large, thriving, successful congregations that need to rediscover a capacity for confession. Within local churches of moderate size and small-membership churches also, confession is not a well-practiced discipline. Forgiveness is not easy to offer or to embrace.

Some years ago, I served a church in a small town where everybody may not have known everybody else, but everybody was only one or two casual conversations away from knowing all they wanted to know about everybody else. In such a context, nearly all families have their children enrolled in the same school system, nearly all use the same health-care providers, nearly all shop at the same few grocery stores, and nearly all can be identified with one of the handful of churches in town. It was in such a setting that a married member of the church came to me for some pastoral counseling. The individual confessed to having had an extramarital affair with another married person. Moreover, the affair had ended unhappily.

The penitent person feared, quite reasonably, that both marriages would be ruined as a result. The person in my office was seeking an environment in which to confess, to seek mercy, to hope for God's forgiveness, and to find a way that might lead to reconciliation.

Such a thing could hardly be confessed in public worship, of course. But in a small town or in a small-membership church there is not likely to be a small group where trusted intimacy would permit such a confession either. The only option seemed to be in private worship. So I counseled the individual to write a prayer of confession, to express what needed to be acknowledged and what needed to be sought in mercy, forgiveness, and absolution through God's grace. We then agreed to meet in the sanctuary of the church, just the two of us, at a time when it was certain no other person would be in the building. Kneeling at the chancel rail, the penitent one read the prayer of confession. Some long silences punctuated the prayer. More silence followed. Then, as the liturgy of the church equips a pastor to say, I offered the words "Hear the good news: Christ died for us while we were yet sinners; that proves God's love toward us. In the name of Jesus Christ, you are forgiven!"[4]

It was a halting, hesitant moment. But it was also a holy one.

The recovery of Methodism will require a deepening awareness of the need to confess our faults, failures, and spiritual emptiness. It will require building time and space for intimacy and trust.

And our confessions will have to involve more than the individual misconduct that arises in sexual indiscretions or violent acts or criminal behavior. There are other forms of sin besides the blatant ones in the second table of the Ten Commandments.

We are still in the process of recovery from Methodism's failures to affirm God's call of women into ministry. The long and difficult story of this grievous error did not come to a conclusion in 1956, with the decision by The Methodist Church to grant women full clergy rights, including ordination and conference membership. It was a failure in the nineteenth century when women were officially denied permission to undertake missions abroad. It was a failure in the nineteenth and twentieth centuries, when women had to struggle for admission as lay members of annual conferences and for election as lay delegates to General Conferences. It was a failure likewise during those same decades when women who had clergy rights within some traditions that eventually merged into The Methodist Church and The United Methodist Church suffered as those authorizations were sacrificed in compromises for the sake of union.

Women are a majority of United Methodist laity but still only slightly more than a third of United Methodist clergy. Women are a majority of the students enrolled in many schools of theology—including United Methodist schools—but a minority of the Boards and District Committees of Ordained Ministry who control the steps toward ordination of seminary graduates. And women in theological school classrooms still are likely to have a sizable majority of their professors be male.

In the nineteenth century, the popular lay preacher and charismatic church leader Phoebe Palmer wondered whether the return of the Lord had been delayed because the church had refused to allow women to proclaim the gospel. In the twentieth and, unhappily, the twenty-first centuries, resistance to women in positions of leadership has continued, albeit in more subtle forms. It includes a reluctance to learn feminist methods of decision making, as well as a resistance to allow collaborative patterns of leadership. It also includes barriers that have been constructed to make maternity leave seem an exception to a career path rather than part of a career path. These are issues in ecclesiastical as well as secular life, of course, but we the church must confess our failure to provide leadership in the world on some of these matters.

There is another issue that needs to be acknowledged and confessed with regard to our understanding of what constitutes Christian ministry. Women, and some men, who have expressed a sense of call to specialized forms of service such as the ministry of scholarship and teaching have been advised not to seek ordination as elders in the church, since pastoral ministry in local congregations tends to be perceived as the norm and other forms of service as aberrations.

This is indeed a peculiar position for Methodists to take, given that the founder of the movement was ordained in a university setting and that most of his ministry was literally in the world that he viewed as his parish. In fact, John Wesley served only one equivalent of a local church in his career, and that was with his father at Wroot, the small community yoked to the parish at Epworth. Otherwise, he held positions as a chaplain in Georgia, an academic fellow of Lincoln College at Oxford, a published scholar, and an itinerant preacher. To insist that the ministry within Methodism be reduced to pastoral work in local congregations as a norm is to exhibit a failure that must be confessed and from which the church must recover.

These matters rather vividly illustrate another issue that must be acknowledged and confessed for the recovery of Methodism—the process by which decisions are made in the church.

In the earliest days of Methodism, it was quite clear. John Wesley made the decisions. He consulted with others, including his brother Charles, but he decided. When he convened his conferences, beginning with the first one in 1744, the "conference" was defined as the persons who gathered for the meeting—not the meeting itself. He decided who the conferees were to be, since he issued the invitations. Hence, he defined the conference.

The agenda for the conference followed a similar pattern. Mr. Wesley would pose the questions for discussion, the conversation would ensue, and then he would express the answers. It was a simple, clear, elegant, authoritarian way to reach conclusions and to do business.

What happened in the latter stages of his life, of course, was that Mr. Wesley realized a new mechanism would have to be empowered to reach decisions. Eventually, he concluded that the conference should have the authority. It was more than an effort to prevent any individual person from usurping authority over the Methodist movement. It was an organizational expression of a theological principle, that one of the means of grace was Christian conferencing.)

Nowadays, conferencing may be practiced in some venues. But it is not likely to occur in the official councils and conferences of the church.

On most topics, ranging from a decision by a local church education committee about the choice of Sunday school curricula to a General Conference action on one of the Social Principles such as abortion or capital punishment, decisions are made by majority vote. That is a splendid, honorable method in a democracy. But it also exposes the fact that, on many if not all items, a potentially sizable and possibly energetic minority holds a dissenting view (or views). On occasion, the minorities feel entirely stifled, as happened recently when a report being prepared for the General Conference by a working group was fashioned in such a way that the finished draft had a clear majority in support of the document and a significant minority opposed to it. Further debate ensued about whether it might be possible to submit both majority and minority reports to the General Conference.

(One of the key principles of democracy is that the majority prevails but the minority is not to be repressed or ignored. Occasionally, however, that principle is overlooked. And that oversight is something else that the church needs to confess.

United Methodism's language in the Social Principles and the legislation in *The Book of Discipline* regarding homosexuality offer a good example. It is clear that a majority prevailed in the adoption of the current statements, and it is also clear that similar majorities have prevailed in approving similar official language for most of the past forty years. It is also clear that the number of dissenting minority voices on these items is considerable. Most of the discussion has occurred along rather rigidly drawn lines. And, where pleas for confession and reconciliation have arisen, they have tended to declare that one side must confess that it is wrong and the other side will receive the repentant opponent as a welcome prodigal returning to the position of truth.

There is, however, an alternate model for decision making. It begins with the premise that flawed human beings with limited human understanding can have deeply held and strongly differing views on a matter. It includes recognition that rarely do conflicts have only two sides—they are far more likely to be multifaceted. Within the branch of Judaism that is identified as Conservative, there is a decision-making body called the Committee on Jewish Law and Standards. It includes thirty people, twenty-five of whom are rabbis with both voice and vote, plus five laypersons who have voice but do not vote. These twenty-five rabbis can reach a majority opinion on some matter with thirteen votes sufficient to declare that a point of view meets Jewish standards. However, if as few as six reach agreement on some point of view, including an alternative point of view, regarding any matter—even a matter on which there is a clear majority—that can also be promulgated as meeting Jewish standards. Hence a majority of thirteen or more could take a position, and a minority of six or more could take a differing or disagreeing position, and both could be recognized as standards in the Conservative tradition. As a result of such a decision-making process, the Jewish Theological Seminary in New York determined that it would admit gay and lesbian applicants for study. At the same time, congregations would have the freedom to choose whether or not to accept gay and lesbian clergy.[5]

The process is not flawless. But, of course, that is the point. No human decision-making process is without flaws. For that reason, a point of view that is held by a significant minority can be judged to have the same legitimacy as the point of view held by a majority. The recovery of Methodism will require a willingness to confess that the church has not yet had the courage to reach such a mature and reasonable conclusion. But doing so, and seeking forgiveness for having failed to do so, will be an important step toward recovery.

An accurate assessment of what ails Methodism and a constructive plan that will lead to the recovery of Methodism must include sincere attitudes and acts of confession about faults and failures. Some of them are personal. Some of them are institutional. All of them are sinful and need healing—the kind that is transforming and renewing. But it will not happen by human wisdom, organizational engineering, systematic restructuring, or majority vote. It will require openness to the mystery of grace.

CHAPTER TWO

When the Positive Is Negative and the Negative Is Positive

"Those who are well have no need of a physician, but those who are sick."

(Matthew 9:12)

On a warm spring day in Dallas, I stopped at a local shop to buy some flowers. It was May 24 on the calendar—Aldersgate Day for those Methodists who pay attention to such things, but more personally for my wife and me, it was our thirty-eighth wedding anniversary.

We had long ago agreed that we would observe the day each year by spending some time together, perhaps going out for a meal at a special place, but not by buying each other gifts. It may have been an echo of something we learned from an older, frugal couple early in our marriage. They marked their anniversary each year by going to a shop and browsing through racks of cards. Each of them would choose what seemed to contain an especially appropriate sentiment and show it to the other with words like these: "If I were going to spend money on a card, this is the one I would give to you." Then they would return the cards to the racks and leave.

Admittedly, my decision to buy some flowers was a violation of that spirit. It was simply a spontaneous, early morning act to choose a bouquet and deliver it to my wife's office. After making a selection, I took the basket to the man at the checkout counter. His comment surprised me.

"Wow," he said, "I hope you didn't do something really bad!"

What I had imagined as a positive, loving action led a stranger to draw an entirely negative conclusion. The flowers were a celebration of thirty-eight years together, not a plea for forgiveness for some heinous act. Nevertheless, a bystander—the clerk at the flower shop—misinterpreted what little information he had and reached a conclusion that was exactly the opposite of what I intended. Happily, my wife accepted the bouquet as a positive act.

But it is true that positives can be read as negatives, and vice versa.

Early in my term as dean of Perkins School of Theology at Southern Methodist University, I was invited to speak at a United Methodist church in central Louisiana. Such opportunities are generous gifts from a pastor or bishop or lay leader, and I try to respond affirmatively to such a request whenever possible. After all, I am an ordained minister, so any invitation to preach the gospel offers an event for fulfilling my vocation. It also has at least the potential to let me meet alumni, talk with prospective students, visit with supporters of the school, and touch the pulse of the church in a local setting.

Despite all the positive aspects of undertaking such a mission, however, there are plenty of negatives. As a visiting preacher, one never knows the context very well. Into what local situation am I intruding? Is it a fulfilling place of ministry for the pastor? Are the laity energized about their sense of mission? Does the church have an investment in, a connection to, a partnership with the local community? Might there be "fightings without and fears within," to borrow a phrase from Charles Wesley?[1]

Unbeknownst to me until I met the pastor of the church on the day before the service, there had been a violent incident in the community just about a week prior to my arrival in town. Police action directed at a perpetrator of an alleged crime had involved gunfire and death. That racial issues were part of the picture became clear—the police officers were white, the individuals whom the police shot were black.

I was scheduled to preach at morning worship and, early in the evening, to participate in an open discussion about theological education for the church's ministries. In between those scheduled activities, some of the church members and their pastor had decided they would attend a community forum that had been hastily arranged to discuss the racial tensions developing as a result of the police action. What would be the mood of the congregation on Sunday morning? What might be the atmosphere in the community after the public forum, just before the evening assembly?

Morning worship followed the pattern that the pastor had predicted. For good or ill, the incident in the community seemed to have little impact on the congregation's life. The evening session offered nothing unexpected either, at least at the start. It unfolded comfortably until, toward the end of the question-and-answer period, a man rose in the back of the sanctuary and said, "I want to tell you what Perkins did to me."

The man, a white fellow who was probably in his seventies, had chosen to begin with words that immediately provoked negative feelings in me. I had been a dean long enough to know that public gatherings like this one give ample opportunity for anyone who has a grievance against the school of theology or the university to voice his or her complaint. His opening words aroused my suspicions right away. My instinctive reaction was to assume the fellow was going to unload his distress about a financial, political, academic, athletic, or spiritual matter at the university. I figured he was unhappy about something, and he was about to let everyone know it.

Moreover, I could feel my body stiffen and my soul become defensive, because when he said, "I want to tell you what Perkins did to me," he started walking down the aisle toward me. Then he stopped and proceeded to tell a story.

After receiving his theology degree from SMU in the early 1960s, he went to his first pastoral appointment in the Louisiana Delta. At that time, the public schools were being integrated. Shortly after he moved into the parsonage and began his ministry, he was approached by a man who revealed that most of the white folks in town were not willing to send their children to school with the black children, adding that a group had been formed to open a private school for white children only. "We need a place to hold classes," the man said, "and Preacher, your church offers the best place in town for our school. So I am asking you to let us use your church during the weekdays as a schoolhouse for our children."

Standing near me amid the gathering in that Louisiana sanctuary, the man with white hair then looked at me and told me what his theological education did to him. He said, "Nobody at Perkins ever taught me how to handle a question like that. No professor at the seminary ever had a course on addressing such things. But here is what Perkins did to me. It gave me a way to think theologically, and it gave me a place to stand. So I stood on that place, looked the man in the eye, and said, 'No.' I told him that he and his group could not use our Methodist church for a segregated school."

When he finished, all of us in the room knew that he had done more than tell a tale about an incident forty years earlier. He had stepped into the midst of a tense and difficult current situation in the community, he had reminded the church that we have to take a stand for a commitment to racial reconciliation, he had used the occasion of my presence to make a legitimate point about theological education for the ministries of the church, and he had turned a potentially negative encounter into a promisingly positive moment.

There is a tendency to assume the worst, to draw the most sinister conclusion, in any occasion. But when it comes to the recovery of the church, we have to be careful never to confuse the negative and the positive. What may look like a rejection of the church can actually be an opportunity for the recovery of Christianity's mission and message. That has been part of the apostolic witness since the founding of the church.

Consider one brief epistle in the New Testament collection that is generally known as "the pastorals." The letter to Titus is one of those tantalizing bits of biblical text that seems strangely incomplete. It clearly appears to be a response to a letter or message from Titus. But we have only the response, not the initial communication. Therefore, readers are forced to draw inferences about the issues raised in the first letter to which Titus is a reply.

Some of the inferences are rather clear. Titus has apparently complained about the miserable situation that he encountered in Crete, the place where he was sent to fulfill his ministry. Rather than dismiss the complaints or suggest that perhaps Titus is overreacting to the difficulties of the assignment, the letter to Titus agrees that problems abound (Titus 1:5-16). It cites the words of one of Crete's own prophets, who noted that "Cretans are always liars, vicious brutes, lazy gluttons." It adds that such "testimony is true." The letter puts even more pejoratives on the pile, calling some people in Crete "detestable, disobedient, unfit for any good work."

The language in the letter to Titus may not be profane or vulgar, but it certainly is harsh. United Methodists have had a lot of nasty things to say about one another in recent years, but rarely if ever has the tone been that brutal—at least in public or in print. If the letter to Titus can be used as a comparison, Methodists have been kind and gentle in describing or caricaturing their foes in the faith.

But all of that coarse, judgmental, negative language in the letter to Titus occurs in a larger, positive context. For the author of the letter, having agreed that the mess in Crete is terrible, insists that Titus was left there precisely because the situation was so bad. "I left you behind in Crete for this reason, so that you should put in order what remained to be done." The message is clear. The negative circumstances are positive opportunities to be seized.

The recovery of Methodism will require hearing that message again. Of course, Methodists have had a long history of doing that. So the recovery of Methodism may be eminently possible. It will simply involve relearning what we have already known—and practiced.

In the middle of the nineteenth century, weary of seeing the social fabric ruined by alcohol abuse, Methodist women in particular rose to the challenge and sought to transform society. The effort that eventually became a campaign for the prohibition of beverage alcohol was not launched simply as a program for imposing some standard for personal morality, but as a mechanism for reshaping social systems. Patterns of domestic abuse, child neglect, and economic waste were the targets of the temperance advocates. Negative circumstances became an occasion for positive mission.

If transforming the social patterns that resulted from substance abuse was a major Methodist program, it was not the only one. Deficiencies in workplace safety prompted Methodists to support the collective bargaining rights of labor. Inadequacies in access to health-care facilities propelled Methodists to open hospitals. Homelessness and neglect affecting children led Methodists to found orphanages and other institutions for child care. Illiteracy and ignorance provoked Methodists to establish schools.

Indeed, among Methodism's particularly distinctive commitments to mission was its focus on education. One of the first institutions that Mr. Wesley created was a school. When bishops Coke and Asbury put their movement into action, they too founded a school. In the decades and centuries that followed, the expanding of educational opportunities was a hallmark of the church's work. From basic instruction to higher education, the movement flourished. Essentially the motivation was societal, not sectarian. It was built upon a conviction that sizable social benefits resulted from developing a better-educated populace. Efforts to educate children and youth came early. The first "seminaries" established by

Methodists, for instance, were not theological schools but elementary and upper-level schools for children and young people where classes were intentionally kept small. They were called "seminaries" because the instruction was conducted in a "seminar" style. Not many of those academies endure. Yet at least one of them—Wyoming Seminary in Pennsylvania—has remained in continuous operation since 1844, enduring across those years despite many challenges including a devastating flood in 1972 that ruined many buildings on campus. Colleges and universities were opened by Methodists during the nineteenth and early twentieth centuries in such vast numbers that the church built nearly as many institutions of higher learning as the Roman Catholic Church—and far more per capita. But more was at stake than simply starting schools. The credibility of the education was important to the church, so it created an accrediting body, the University Senate.

Currently, more than a hundred colleges and universities are affiliated with The United Methodist Church. Most are no longer owned, controlled, or dominated by the denomination, yet that alone is testimony to the importance the church placed on offering institutions of higher learning for the benefit of the larger society rather than the statistical expansion of the church. The needs of the society, not the needs of the church, were the real motivation for this endeavor. If there were deficiencies in the social order, the church felt prompted to act in constructive ways. Negative circumstances were not viewed as cause for despair but as occasions for positive action.

Such things still happen.

When a gunman killed several young Amish girls in their school building near a Pennsylvania farm, the reaction that galvanized people around the world was not solely shared grief at the senseless deaths of the children, but also shared awe at the capacity of the Amish community to demonstrate forgiveness. The widow of the gunman was embraced by support from the victims' families. Representatives of the Amish community attended her late husband's funeral. In the wake of violence, the sect demonstrated the power that can be expressed in acts of mercy and reconciliation.

Because of its highly sectarian nature, the Amish community is easily identified. Its population is highly concentrated in a small number of select areas. So its public acts of faithful witness, though infrequent, are highly visible. Methodists are far more widely dispersed throughout North American culture. Not only are they harder to identify, they are potentially invisible. There is nothing distinctive in Methodists' attire, for instance.

But is there anything distinctive about Methodists' actions? Is there any social challenge that might offer an opportunity for Methodism to recover its capacity for a distinctive public voice?

A case in point might involve the current struggles within the lower forty-eight United States regarding immigration. The negative aspects of this situation abound and exist on all sides of the conservative/liberal debate. Like most conflicted issues, there are not two sides to this impasse. There are many. Yet various forces want to frame the discussion in the starkest and simplest terms as a pro or con, liberal or conservative set of issues.

The arguments appear to take uncompromising positions. Some argue that it is strictly an issue of legal versus illegal immigration. Some argue that it is actually a matter of supply and demand within the labor market, where immigrants (regardless of whether their "papers" are legal) offer to work in jobs that are not being taken by indigenous residents or citizens. Some argue that it is merely a matter of humane concern for children (some now grown to maturity) who were brought into the United States by their families and who cannot or should not be held accountable for any illegal entry that their parents may have perpetrated. Some argue that it is really a matter of national security, to protect the borders of the United States from incursion by terrorists. Some argue that it is solely a practical matter of public health to provide for the health and welfare of all persons, with no discrimination based on residential status or ability to pay, because the public at large is better served by treating those who are ill so as to avoid the spread of communicable diseases. Some maintain that the arguments against tolerant treatment of undocumented—or illegal—immigrants are rationalizations serving to layer a veneer of civility over racism and ethnocentrism. It is worth noting that the only place a fence or wall is being constructed is along the border between the United States and Mexico, not along the much longer and much more porous border between the United States and Canada.

But what do Methodists argue? Well, the answer is "All of the above." There is no distinguishable Methodist or United Methodist point of view on immigration matters. What Methodists may assert is embedded and disbursed across the broad spectrum of discussion throughout North America. In effect, the Wesleyan tradition and the Methodist movement have let their witness disappear into the landscape. It is unheard as well as unseen.

The recovery of Methodism will require more than gathering the loose fragments of various points of view that may be held by Methodists who are indistinguishable from the other features on the political horizon. And the recovery of Methodism will require more than restoring some historic theme that prevailed in past eras of immigration debate. The recovery of Methodism will require a method for renewing its distinctive presence in addressing the conflicts in North America concerning immigration. The environment now is one in which the voices of the faithful, signifying hope for redeeming and transforming the world, cannot clearly be discerned from the voices of the faithless, whose arguments are filled with sound and fury, yet signify nothing. Negative answers seem to be the only responses available. The recovery of Methodism requires rediscovering the message of redemption.

But it is not easy to overcome the negative impulse. Whether bigotry is the basis of it or not, fear is real. And there are many reinforcements for surrendering to our fears.

In the months following the attacks on September 11, 2001, air travel was slow to recover. And I was one of the travelers who took a while before planning a trip by plane. My first involved a cross-country trek to attend an academic meeting. For scheduling reasons, my trip from west to east took place in the evening. We boarded the plane before sunset and flew through dusk into darkness. The vast majority of the seats on the plane were empty, as was typical in those uncertain days. Any passenger who wanted a row of three seats to himself or herself could have it and could lie down for a nap.

After we had been airborne for long enough that the sky was totally dark, I heard the passenger in the row behind me summon a flight attendant. "May I help you?" In the darkness, I heard the male voice of the passenger ask the female flight attendant, "Which way is east?" After a pause, she said, "I beg your pardon?" He asked again, "Which way is east?" She answered, "Just a moment, I will check with the pilot."

I had noticed the man as he boarded the plane shortly after me. A swarthy fellow with a beard, he appeared to be a man of Arabic ancestry.

My instincts told me that the flight attendant was indeed going to consult the pilot, but not for the purpose of checking directions. We were on an airplane that was heading from the West Coast to the East Coast of the United States, so it was obvious that east was directly in front of the nose of the aircraft. Why did he need to know which way was east? My anxieties were rising palpably. Was this going to be a post–9/11 moment? A host of negative thoughts and feelings became nearly overwhelming.

The flight attendant returned and spoke to the passenger. She told him that we were heading due east, so east was directly in front of the plane. He thanked her for the information. A few minutes later, I heard him get out of his seat and head toward the rear of the aircraft. The tension grew. Many minutes of quiet followed. I decided to walk toward the rear of the plane and visit the restroom. About two-thirds of the way back, I passed the galley area—an open space where airline personnel prepare their carts for the beverage service. It was unoccupied, except for a swarthy, bearded man who had spread a carpet and was kneeling in prayer.

That was when my anxieties turned to guilt. The person whom I allowed myself to fear was not a threat or a negative presence at all. He clearly was a devout Muslim who was not about to let a designated hour for prayer pass without devotion. Being in a plane was not an excuse to neglect the distinctive practices of his religion. I, on the other hand, had let my fears trump my faith. I had permitted a negative perception of the situation to overwhelm any positive interpretation of the facts. I had not turned to some ritual for evening prayer to cope with the worries of the moment. At least a confession of sinfully weak faith seemed appropriate. So I offered that and hoped for forgiveness.

The recovery of Methodism will require a distinctive set of practices devoted to a deep sense of hope. But some circumstances are a challenge to hope.

On a comfortable winter afternoon, I received a call from a physician with the results of a biopsy. He informed me that the lab report was positive. What that meant for me personally was that the news was negative. The biopsy revealed that I had prostate cancer.

Within a few days, he said, my wife and I would need to visit with him in his office to discuss the diagnostic details and the treatment options. It proved to be more than a week until we met with him. And during those intervening days, I found myself living in a strange world. For one thing, I scarcely felt ill at all. My tumor was a rather unobtrusive potential killer. Physical examinations, lab tests, and the definitive biopsy had found the disease. But, as I said to many persons who asked, I have felt far more ill with a bad cold or the flu than I did with cancer. There had been no overt symptoms that interfered significantly with my life.

Nevertheless, the word "cancer" is about as troubling a set of syllables as one can hear applied to oneself. When I awakened in the night—and most men of a certain age do so, with or without prostate cancer—I became conscious of uncontrollably disturbing questions. What are those little cancer cells doing while I lie in bed trying to sleep? Will I get to see my granddaughter or her soon to be born sibling grow beyond preschool years? Will I be able to continue working? Must my wife and I rethink our long-term plans? How will I tell the truth to my mother? Is the promise of eternal resurrection as real as the presence of the deadly disease in my body?

What's more, all of the questions were not merely internal issues arising within me. I lead a reasonably public life, one that does not allow a major illness to be merely a private or a personal matter. I had official obligations to fulfill, including two dinners that my wife and I were scheduled to host for members of the Perkins faculty and their guests at our home. We decided to proceed with the dinner plans, and I chose to meet as many of my calendared commitments as possible before my medical treatment began. Further, I chose to be as public as possible within the Perkins School of Theology and my annual conference about the details of the diagnosis and treatment. The rumor mill would, of course, carry the information more widely.

My wife and I shared the news with a couple of our neighbors. Beyond them, we trusted our community's grapevine to spread the news. It did not take long. Besides, our streets had plenty of experience in dealing with deadly diseases. Two days before the doctor called with my diagnosis, I conducted a funeral for our neighbor who had died of lung cancer. A year before that, another neighbor succumbed to a similar disease. And, apparently, word about my situation traveled fast. On the night when my wife and I hosted one of our faculty dinners, a guest who arrived a few minutes late had to park several blocks from our house. As he walked around the corner, one of our neighbors came out of her front door toward him. She had noticed all of the people who were heading to our home, and she put a question to the faculty member about me: "Did he die?"

It was a dinner party that had brought all the vehicles to the neighborhood, not a wake. Of course, only a few persons in nearby houses actually knew that. As is often the case, when real information is not available, people assume the negative.

And yet, despite the diagnosis, despite the information that was being ground out by the rumor mill, I kept listening to the word from my doctor. "I am going to cure you," he said, "and you are going to live for years and years and years."

There is a tendency to interpret the signs of our times in the most negative terms. Of course, there are plenty of reasons to do so. The first decade of the twenty-first century may offer the last chance to prevent the most feared and most catastrophic consequences of global warming. Epidemiologists are pondering the possibility of a global pandemic, caused by bird flu. The largest and most powerful economy in the world—that of the United States—is increasingly dependent on oil controlled by uncontrollable forces, and that economic vigor has been built on a national debt of unfathomable proportions.

A search for security and serenity in the midst of these fears leads in many different directions. One involves bigger, fiercer, nastier weapons. Another involves building walls to separate nations and groups (Palestine and Israel, the United States and Mexico). Another involves spiritual quests.

Methodism appears less and less often to be one of those spiritual options—at least, not a particularly distinctive one. And many who look at the situation of the church today read the evidence negatively as well.

CHAPTER THREE

Methodism Under a Microscope

"For now we see in a mirror, dimly."
(1 Corinthians 13:12)

Occasionally we use the metaphor of a looking glass to help us explain things. Is it a window through which we look upon the world, or a mirror in which we see only the reflection of ourselves? Or thinking about the glass in a car, one asks whether we are looking at the church through the windshield—with a focus on the future toward which we are heading—or the rearview mirror, which only helps us see where we have been. I hope to look through a different kind of lens—namely, a microscope, which allows us to focus on the small things, the normally unseen things.

Some things about United Methodism in the United States are obvious to anyone who cares to notice. The declines in membership are steady, though relatively small, in numerical terms. But they are precipitous in comparison to changes in population. The aging demographic profile of the denomination is clear. The regions of the country where United Methodism seems to be statistically strong are in the southern sections of the country—from the

Mason-Dixon Line to the Gulf of Mexico, and from the Atlantic Ocean to the Texas panhandle. Elsewhere, there are few signs of strength. The number of persons being ordained elder is growing smaller, compared with the number of elders who are retiring. The number of appointments being served by part-time pastors and by persons without full clergy credentials is growing. The costs of funding health insurance and retirement accounts are becoming increasingly burdensome.

But macro-management does not help us. Is a church relatively weak because it has few—or fewer—worshipers entering the doors every Sunday? Is a church relatively strong if it has packed pews and prospering programs?

I conducted a consultation with a local United Methodist church in North Carolina some years ago. By all evidence it was a thriving operation. People were driving either a few miles or, in some cases, many miles to attend worship every week. There was a warm and friendly fellowship among the members. There were no symptoms of trouble or unhappiness or conflict.

When one looked at the small details under a microscope, however, a different picture emerged. The fact that people were driving to the church, some from great distances, was a clue that the church was having little relationship with or impact upon its local community. The warm and friendly fellowship masked an unseen fact about the congregation—its lack of diversity was a clue that only people of a certain viewpoint or a certain generational cohort or a certain cultural subgroup were truly welcome. The occupied pews conveyed the impression that this was a lively, growing church, but its numerical growth was not keeping pace with the population growth in the immediate area. In short, the church was in trouble, though it was experiencing no obvious symptoms of trouble. Only by examining it carefully, under a microscope, could the problems be found, acknowledged, treated, and resolved.

A more closely focused study of the denomination as a whole is also revealing. It yields the identification of four factors that have created problems for Methodism. These four are the congregationalization of the church, the identification of American Methodism with the North American middle class, the acceptance of secular political categories as a way to understand the church, and the tendency to transmute the art of ministry into the management of ministry. Each of these four deserves a reasonably detailed look.

Congregationalization

The first of these factors can be called the congregationalization of the church.

For most of its first 150 years in North America, Methodism understood itself as a missionary movement that was broadly connected. Its system of conferences—quarterly, annual, and general—offered an interlocking set of relationships that provided guidance and governance for the cause. The nineteenth century was a time of great ferment and productivity for the movement. Numerous denominational divisions occurred. At the same time, new institutions formed. One organizational unit that became increasingly significant was known by a term that Methodists had resisted using: "local church."

The very notion of "location" was nearly anathema to early Methodism. When preachers no longer could continue in the active, itinerant ministry, what they did was "locate." It is still the case that United Methodism's official jargon for ordained ministers is to call them "traveling preachers." When an ordained minister reaches the point, either professionally or vocationally, that continuing in the itinerant ministry is no longer an option, one possibility is to take the step into "honorable location." That way, she or he no longer has traveling orders but has only limited authorizations to conduct the acts of ministry within a pastoral charge where the individual has located. The term "local pastor" still officially means, in The United Methodist Church, a person who has been authorized to conduct certain acts of ministry within the limits of a charge to which she or he has been appointed.

What bishops did, when they were fulfilling their constitutional responsibilities, was "travel" throughout the connection. In fact, they were not known as resident bishops for they did not reside in a particular place. They could live anywhere they wished. They would preside at various conferences of the church. But they had no designated location.

Increasingly, however, the word "local" has lost its meaning as a withdrawal from the full exercise of ordained ministry and has acquired meaning as the principal place for the exercise of ministry. One could see the emergence of this phenomenon with the rising significance of sizable and strong local churches in the nineteenth century. Gradually, such connectional institutions as camp meetings and quarterly conferences weakened, and congregations widened their place in the denomination. In the 1920s, both primary bodies of American Methodism—the Methodist Episcopal Church and the Methodist Episcopal Church, South—began using the phrase "local church" in their *Disciplines*. Earlier generations of Methodists who were formally received into membership became members first of the connection and secondarily members of a local body. Subsequent generations of Methodists were told that they were joining a congregation that was affiliated or linked to the rest of the denomination. Pastors even modified the official language for receiving members, asking the "loyalty" question by inserting a few words: "Will you be loyal to *this congregation of* The United Methodist Church and uphold it by your prayers, your presence, your gifts, and your service?" By the late twentieth century, United Methodist *Disciplines* were identifying local churches as the primary places where the church encounters the world.

Some of the facets of this transition have been subtle. Others have not. Ordained Methodists have always served in a variety of connectional settings for ministry. They have been military chaplains, university professors, denominational executives, roving evangelists, and leaders of institutional ministries, just to name a few. Some of them have presented unusual challenges to the church. For example, in the 1970s, a clergy member of the Eastern Pennsylvania Conference who was serving as pastor of a local church was elected to Congress. Yet, as Bishop James Mase Ault noted at the time, the church did not provide a category in the *Discipline* for appointing an ordained minister to the United States House of Representatives.[1]

But as the church crafted language for the full range of places in which ordained persons might serve with the authorization of the church, they came collectively to be known as "appointments beyond the local church." Thus, the proper and privileged type of appointment for an ordained woman or man was judged to be pastoral service in a congregational setting. Any other form of activity looked like a deviation from the norm.

With the emergence in 1996 of the Order of Deacon as a category for full clergy members of an annual conference to be acknowledged as fully ordained ministers, there was also a need to recognize that some deacons (as well as some elders) exercise their vocations in secular work rather than ecclesiastical functions. The phrase "appointment beyond the local church" was altered to "appointment to extension ministry." Yet the message remained that such activities were, in effect, extending the ministries of local churches—which remained normative—into broader arenas.

During the same period, advocates of long-term pastorates became persuasive. The earliest Methodist itinerants rarely traveled the same circuit for more than a year. By the first half of the twentieth century, the standard length of appointment to a charge was four consecutive years. But pressures mounted to recognize that stability in the pastoral leadership of a local church seemed to be consistent with church growth. Pastoral terms of five to seven years in one setting became the goal. Career-long ministries in one place, like Ralph Sockman's forty-four years at Christ Church Methodist[2] in New York City, have remained a rarity. But appointments enduring for twenty or twenty-five years—especially in larger congregations—became increasingly common. This has had a reinforcing effect on the notion that the basic institution of the denomination is the local church, notwithstanding the clear stipulation in the constitution of The United Methodist Church that the basic unit of the church is the annual conference.

The congregationalization of the church has occurred in forms other than terms of pastoral leaders. Increasingly, local churches have exercised the freedom to devise their own systems of local governance. In the past, it had been possible connectionally to identify and encourage lay officers in local settings who held comparable responsibilities for education, worship, evangelism, and other program areas. More recent restructurings have exercised freedom in local churches and have made such connections harder to sustain.

Further atomization of Methodism into its congregational fragments has occurred with the recruitment and deployment of church staff. In congregations with multiple staff members assigned to specific program areas, personnel committees and senior ministers use their own recruitment devices and hiring practices to bring specialized professionals into their leadership team. Ordained or lay, Methodist or not, such professionals tend to be task-directed rather than mission-driven. Their performances are assessed locally not connectionally. Their identification is with a congregation not with a movement.

While it may be possible to determine that these developments have enhanced the profile of individual congregations, it can also be argued that these developments have at least accompanied—if not caused—the decline in the denomination. Attention to local churches as the preeminent institutional forms of church life needs reexamination under a microscope. Unless Methodists are eager and willing for their movement to become a loose confederation of congregations, the recovery of Methodism will require renewing and transforming a sense of connection.

Middle-Classism

There is a second factor that comes into view when one looks at Methodism under a microscope. It is the church's identification with the North American middle class. Some time ago, historian Kenneth Rowe characterized the trend in nineteenth-century Methodism as a move from the backstreet to the main street. There is no doubt that by cultural and economic classifications, Methodists are predominantly a middle-class body.

Within the United States, that immediately creates certain problems. Every issue that is important to, or divisive within, the middle class of North Americans becomes an issue of importance or division for Methodists. Most of the debates and compromises about the Social Principles mirror the discussions in the middle of American society. For the most part, to attend a Methodist congregation is to wear the clothing, drive the cars, and adhere to the tastes of middle-class Americans. Whether that is an aesthetic problem is not the issue. More seriously, it may be a theological and missional problem.

For one thing, a focus upon and an identification with the broad middle of the culture omits two very significant groups of God's people. One is the poor. The other is the rich.

A sizable amount of theological and missional attention has been given in recent decades to the gospel mandate to bring good news to the poor. Phrases have entered the language of the church, like God's preferential option for the poor, which are biblically based and historically consistent with the witness of the faith. No one can study the career of John Wesley and overlook his commitment to the poor. Denominational institutions have devoted themselves to the needs of the poor, from providing health care to those who cannot pay for the services, to providing financial aid for students in higher education, to providing food service and shelter that otherwise would not be available to impoverished persons.

Yet the question always remains whether this is largesse to the poor or inclusion within the church of the poor. That will happen only when the needs of the poor are as integral to the mission of the church as are the interests of the middle class. Does health care for those who lack it command the same attention as the music program or the youth ministry or the child-care services that a local church provides. Does the public or private education of children in impoverished households remain as sharply focused as the education of middle-class children? Are church suppers as routinely provided for feeding the poor as they are for the fellowship of the comfortable?

Nowhere has this problem been more apparent in recent years than in the strategy for church growth through new congregational development that Methodists have used. In too many regions, church planting has been less an exercise in evangelism than it has been in real estate. The approach has been to find a place— typically a new, suburban subdivision—where population is expected to increase. Then funding is provided to get a congregation started, with the provision that it must be a financially self-sustaining local church in some relatively short time, such as three to five years. As Justo González[3] has pointed out, this is not a strategy for delivering the gospel to people who need Methodism but a strategy for making the church available to people who can afford Methodism. At its base, this has been a device for enhancing the denomination's embrace of the middle class, the people who can afford mortgages and automobiles and retail prices at shopping malls.

Meanwhile, there is another group Methodists have tended to overlook, though they are a class that Jesus did not ignore any more than the poor. These are the people of substantial wealth and high incomes. The amount of attention Jesus gave to the wealthy gets relatively little notice.

To be sure, he did say that it was easier for a rich man to go through the eye of a needle than to enter the kingdom of heaven. But he also said, in the parable of the talents, that the frightened and frugal man with one talent, who buried it rather than put it in an interest-bearing savings account, should have it taken away and given to the man with the most money. In his parable of the laborers in the vineyard, it is the rich landowner who chooses to compensate everyone with a full day's pay that becomes a sign of grace.

In the parable of the prodigal son, it is the father—a man rich enough to withstand the waste of significant wealth—who provides a warm welcome for his wayward son, gives him a robe, donates a valued ring, kills a fatted calf for an impromptu feast, and still has enough left to leave a substantial bequest to an older, hardworking son. That father becomes a sign of mercy.

But the rich can be made to feel uncomfortable in the church also. If they are perceived, as is too often the case, as the financial fountains to whom the church will turn for every budget shortfall or building need, then they cease to be treated as full partners in the life and ministries of the church. Moreover, stewardship education has been a weak aspect of the denomination's life for a long time. The wealthy are more aware than anyone else about the spiritual and emotional problems that accompany great financial resources. Benevolence as a principle is laudable but, as a practice, it is a challenge. John D. Rockefeller Jr. made it his full-time job. Andrew Carnegie, whose acquisition of wealth was hardly noble, devoted a significant part of his life to giving it away. But how much should be given? And to whom should it be offered? And for what should it be committed? Such questions have rarely been pondered in a theological and missional context by the church. And people of wealth should be part of the consultation.

The recovery of Methodism will require reconnecting with multiple classes of society, especially with the poor and rich.

Bisection

A third factor that has created problems for Methodism is a tendency to be absorbed into the political categories of the culture by embracing the notion that there are two sides to every issue. The notion that all searches for truth can be fulfilled by a bisection of each topic is actually an impediment to the search for truth. On almost every important topic there are not two sides but many facets. Settling for such categories as conservative and liberal, right and left, red and blue, or progressive and regressive will scarcely begin to grasp the complexities of most matters. But in a political context that has decided to adopt a point-counterpoint approach to debate, the church has seemed willing for the sake of convenience to take the same approach.

During my first full-time appointment as a pastor in the early 1970s, I became acquainted with an organization called the Clergy Consultation Service. Founded by a group of pastors in New York City and elsewhere, the service recruited pastors who were willing to volunteer some of their time for counseling women who were facing what they considered to be problem pregnancies. For those who volunteered, the service gave training in the art of counseling women in these complex circumstances. In addition, the service maintained a list of referral options that included adoption, support for single parenthood, and abortion choices. It offered a sense of safety and freedom to women who, before the Supreme Court decision known as *Roe v. Wade*, had few if any safe or legal alternatives.

There were then, as there are now, forces and voices who want to reduce the discussion about abortion to two clear alternatives. But my experiences in counseling a number of women of every imaginable childbearing age made it clear that there were not two sides to the abortion debate. The actual number may not be countless, but it is very large. My counselees included a rape victim whose pregnancy resulted from an act of violence, a prostitute whose pregnancy was a professional inconvenience, a wife with three young children and a husband who had just lost his job, a mistress whose lover abandoned her as soon as he learned about her pregnancy, and a woman whose youngest child was in his twenties and who could not face the physical or emotional demands of bearing or raising another child. None of these women were a debating point. All of them were complex human beings trying to cope with extraordinarily difficult situations. One or two had an entirely amoral attitude toward the pregnancy. Almost all struggled deeply with moral questions in an ethical crisis.

None were helped by having the issue bisected into sides that were strictly pro-life or pro-choice. Those are merely artificial debating positions. They are not the real human circumstances in which decisions must be made or ministries must be exercised.

On the even more intensely debated topic of homosexuality, much of the church discussion has now settled into an argument over what should or should not be codified into ecclesiastical law. It is as if the denomination were being asked to determine, by a set of majority votes, what is the legally binding Methodist position concerning clergy and laity in the church. But to pursue such a goal is actually to seek the rejection, rather than the recovery, of Methodism. For the church is a connectional body whose deliberations and decisions are made by conferences linked to one another. It is not a hierarchical unit whose legislative or juridical actions are imposed with authority.

I have been a pastor of United Methodist churches during each of the decades that the denominational debate over homosexuality has raged. In every congregation I have served, there have been gay and lesbian members. In the annual conferences with whose members I have become acquainted, there are ordained ministers who are gay and lesbian. Among the candidates for ordained ministry whom local United Methodist churches encourage to attend seminary and pursue a call to ministry, there are gay and lesbian men and women. A hierarchical system can try to impose a single legislative will on its constituency. Or a congregational system can live with the flexibility that legislation for the denomination cannot restrain a local church's right to decide its own policies and practices. But connectional life, as is the case with the polity of Methodism, must find another way. The majority on any topic may decide, but it cannot dictate.

The real issue is that if the church bisects every item into political determinations about majority and minority points of view, then it is surrendering its theological process of discernment in order to achieve a political decision. That is what the secular world wants the church to do, for then it can conveniently label Methodism as conservative or liberal.

The recovery of Methodism will require changing the paradigm of the church's language from the political to the theological.

Management

A fourth factor that has created problems for Methodism is the tendency to transmute the art of ministry into the management of ministry. Creativity and spirituality manifest the mysteries of the faith in painting and poetry, movement and music, speech and silence. Seeking to make all of that more manageable is a limiting and reductionist activity.

There are numerous examples of this in the life of the church. I will cite only three.

First, there has been a growing interest in seeking to manage our doctrine. One of the hallmarks of Methodism in general is that, for most of our history, we have resisted an impulse to turn our teachings into a manageable and enforceable code. Every time we have tried to certify specific sources as the only authoritative body of teaching, we have provoked debate but not decision. Are the legitimate sources of Methodist doctrine in the materials from Mr. Wesley his *Sermons* and *Notes on the New Testament*? Or do they include his abridgment of the *Articles of Religion*? What about the various *Minutes* of the conferences? Do the four sources and guidelines for reaching theological judgments (the so-called Wesleyan Quadrilateral) actually come from Wesley or are they inferences that can be drawn from Wesley and be differently interpreted? And, while all of those issues continue to grow in a mounting pile, who decides what are the correct answers? There is no Methodist equivalent of the Roman Congregation for Sacred Doctrine or the Lambuth Conference for the Anglicans.

What Methodism has are conferences. Though these bodies do legislative and administrative work, theologically they are means of grace. That means their activities are part of the ongoing, organic life of the church whose decisions are by definition the imperfect results of a process for giving and receiving grace from one another. For that reason, Methodists have resisted efforts to turn church doctrine into a manageable code that can be applied and enforced. When clergy are received into conference membership and are asked a set of "historic questions," they are asked whether they have studied "our doctrines," whether they believe our doctrines to be in accord with the Scriptures, and whether they will teach and maintain these doctrines. But, in that public examination, they are not asked to list those doctrines. Similarly, when lay members are received into local churches, they may be asked to renounce wickedness and evil, to accept God's gifts of freedom and power, and to confess Jesus Christ as Lord. But they are not required to pass a test on the teachings of the church.

That is not an oversight on the part of Methodism. It is an indication that we do not require members to stipulate the specifics of church doctrine. Rather, we invite them to sing it. The primary theological textbook for Methodist people in general has been the hymnal.

We should adhere to that approach again. The recovery of Methodism will not occur by making the teachings of the faith more manageable but by making their mysteries more accessible through the music that lets us sing it and the conferencing that graciously enables us to share it.

Second, there has been a growing desire to manage the operations of ministry. In a search for metaphors and models, we have done what generations of Christians in other centuries have done. We have looked to the surrounding culture for suggestions. The role of a tribal elder, for example, could be useful in constructing a job description for an ordained elder. Or duties of a pastor could be drawn from the responsibilities of a shepherd caring for a flock. In more recent times, there has been an increasing amount of appreciation for the notion of the minister as a leader, perhaps as a servant leader, perhaps as an executive leader modeled on those successful in the corporate world.

All such models have their inadequacies, of course. But common to them all is the fact that ministry is more than any of those things. To be ordained, in one description of the office, is to be a steward of the mysteries of God. To preside at the administration of the sacraments and to proclaim the message of the gospel in prophetic sermons are not mechanical or manageable actions. They are passageways linking the mysterious and the mundane. This is not to suggest that persons in ministry should settle for being less than visionary leaders. But it is to insist that it is vital to know where that vision originates and to whom any visionary minister is accountable for pursuing it. As Ernest T. Campbell has written, "We can all confess to a tendency to retreat from the mysterious to the manageable."[4]

Third, we have tried to manage ministry by manipulating the symbols of the faith.

When I was chair of an annual conference Board of Ordained Ministry, I had a major responsibility for the logistics of the ordination service. The bishop wanted all of the clergy to robe and to march in the procession that began the service. Every pastor was to dress in the regalia that she or he customarily wore to lead worship.

The fact that this meant a variety of robes, albs, suits, cassocks, and surplices in the procession actually brought plenty of diversity to the experience. It was a problem, however, that clergy who were not ordained elders[5] wore their accustomed worship attire, which often included a robe or an alb and a stole.

The climactic moments in the ritual came with the physical acts that were directed toward each ordinand. First was the act of laying hands upon her or him, beginning with the bishop and continuing with the hands of others who were assisting in the action. Second was the imposition of a stole, which the bishop placed as a yoke around the neck and shoulders of the person being ordained—looking at each person directly and saying, "You are yoked to Christ and to Christ forever." But the symbol was deprived of much of its meaning, for plenty of individuals who were not yet ordained had marched in the opening procession while wearing their stoles and plenty of those being ordained had already been wearing stoles for a long time as decorative devices.

During the production of the movie based on the novel *The Da Vinci Code*, a sound track was added with music that was intended to suggest medieval Latin. But it was actually a set of freely sung syllables that were deliberately created to convey an impression of Latin, without carrying any meaning whatsoever.

There are churches that nowadays avoid using the symbols of the faith—cross, pulpit, font, table—so as not to offend any attendee who considers such physical signs to be troubling or perplexing. The recovery of Methodism will require a renewed awareness of the mysteries of the faith that are conveyed in symbol because they cannot be managed or manipulated into meaninglessness.

CHAPTER FOUR

A Fear of Fractures

"Do you think that I have come to bring peace to the earth?
No, I tell you, but rather division!"
(Luke 12:51)

Near the close of United Methodism's General Conference in 2004, a tumultuous event rocked the delegates gathered in Pittsburgh. Some individuals, apparently linked to a certain advocacy group, circulated a proposal that the denomination should begin having earnest conversations about an "amicable separation" into two or more parts. The delegates reacted swiftly, affirming their love for one another and endorsing the unity of the church in a resolution that passed with an overwhelming margin of nine to one.

Of the fears that bedevil the denomination, one of the most serious seems to be that it might fracture into separate pieces.

The broader ecclesiastical situation contributes to such fears. For one thing, The United Methodist Church was formed in a decade that was celebrating ecumenical unity. On a global level, the Roman Catholic Church had conducted its Vatican Council in a way that seemed to open doors that had heretofore been closed, and the World Council of Churches had established a basis for interchurch conversation through its document "Baptism, Eucharist, and Ministry." On a denominational level, efforts including the Consultation on Church Union were drawing major Protestant groups together around a vision that dared to imagine an end to ecclesiastical boundaries. And, on a local level, many different kinds of interchurch activities, prayer services, experimental liturgies, and shared practices were being developed on an unprecedented scale.

But the ensuing decades opened fissures within and between ecclesial bodies. The vision fostered by the Consultation on Church Union foundered. Later statements from Rome seemed to emphasize those aspects of the documents from Vatican II that affirmed the primacy of Peter and the hegemony of the Roman Catholic Church. Such things had been conveniently ignored in headier days, but they came back into focus by the dawn of the twenty-first century. The worldwide Anglican Communion, which is built upon the links between national church bodies and the Archbishop of Canterbury, faced open rebellion over the consecration of an openly homosexual bishop, with some parishes in the United States withdrawing completely from the Episcopal Church and other parishes seeking links outside the United States through other national churches to Canterbury. More than one parish in Virginia looked to Anglican bishops in African countries for their episcopal supervision. Still more parishes tried to establish direct ties to Canterbury, bypassing a regional diocese and any national leadership altogether.

Meanwhile, the very idea of a denomination was beginning to appear archaic and obsolete. References to a post-denominational age became commonplace. Churches that boldly declared themselves to be "nondenominational" took shape on the ecclesiastical landscape. Large congregations within denominations increasingly showed willingness to function with indifference toward their judicatories. Congregations, instead of waiting for their denominations to start new churches, provided the energy and resources to plant new communities of faith. A publication called *The Church Report* named the five most influential congregations in the United States, and all of them—Willow Creek in Illinois, Saddleback in California, North Point in Georgia, Fellowship in Grapevine, Texas, and Lakewood in Houston—are independent bodies with thousands of attendees each week, with millions of followers around the country, and with no identifiable ties to any church organization or denomination except themselves and the networks they create.

Alliances became issue-driven not institution-driven. A major program officer for the Southern Baptists announced that on specific issues such as abortion and homosexuality, his church had more in common with the Roman Catholic Church than with most other Protestant bodies.

It is within this context that Methodism—including United Methodism—faces possibilities of its own fracturing. On some public and political issues, it is clear that there are United Methodist clergy and congregations who would be more comfortable with certain Baptists and Catholics than with other United Methodists. On some strategic issues concerning church leadership styles, there are Methodists who are more likely to see the pastoral leaders of large independent churches as better mentors than anyone in their own denomination. In very large congregations, where a few thousand attend worship every week, there will be a greater sense of affinity with churches of similar size than with churches of a similar denominational brand or doctrinal heritage.

Perhaps one reason not to fear the prospect of fracturing is that, on an operational level, it has already occurred. Denominational relationships, if they matter at all, are not primary in the lives of many congregations and clergy. One can see it in the choices that many individuals and institutions of the church are making with regard to the theological education of future leaders. Region is a far more important factor than denomination.

In the western part of Pennsylvania, Methodists are as likely to consider enrolling at a Presbyterian seminary in Pittsburgh as they are to travel to a United Methodist school in Ohio or New Jersey. In the central part of Texas, candidates for ordained ministry will look to a Disciples of Christ institution in Fort Worth rather than to United Methodist schools in Dallas or Kansas City.

And these decisions are often supported, if not actively encouraged, by leaders of the denomination. Boards of ordained ministry in a number of annual conferences distribute their available financial aid dollars equally to all of their seminary students regardless of whether those candidates for the ordained ministry are attending Methodist institutions or schools tied to other traditions. Cabinets are inviting candidates for the ordained ministry to consider accepting appointments to congregations and serving as student local pastors and attending seminaries closer to the local church appointment than a more distant United Methodist theological school.

On a functional level, there is plenty of fracturing in Methodist life. That is one reason not to fear it, perhaps, since it is already a reality.

There is another reason as well. To be afraid of fracturing seems disingenuous for Methodists, who have broken and fragmented multiple times.

The history of Methodism is a history of breaking apart, amicably and otherwise. Separation from the authority of the movement in Britain was only the beginning. Later fractures occurred almost routinely. Divisions took place over major as well as minor issues, over personal as well as prophetic struggles. Many of the separated fragments kept using a label like Methodist or Wesleyan in their new organizational titles, since the end of unity did not deprive any of the enduring fragments of their heritage. Black Methodists who felt forced out of the Methodist connection were still Methodists, and they rightfully insisted upon that identity in the African Methodist Episcopal and African Methodist Episcopal Zion churches. In the same way, black Methodists who were carved out of the Methodist Episcopal Church, South, to form the Colored Methodist Episcopal Church were still Methodists. The democratic impulse motivated Methodist Protestants to create "a church without a bishop for a country without a king," but they were still Methodists. National boundaries shaped Methodism in many places such as Mexico,

Argentina, and Korea. Colonial ties shaped Methodism in other places such as Liberia and Kenya. But they were still Methodists.

There have been breakups and breakdowns aplenty in the history of Methodism. Most dramatic in the United States was the split that was formally negotiated in 1844, tearing the primary Methodist body into northern and southern units. And even when long conversations about reunion culminated in the recovery from nearly a century of separation, the new Methodist Church broke itself into jurisdictions whose principal (if not sole) reason for existing was to maintain segregation by race.

Curiously, that century of separation was perhaps the most effective period of Methodism's life in North America. Global mission activity was energized. Women, officially denied the opportunity to serve abroad, formed their own mission-sending organization. Institutions for the transformation of society were created. As Sarah Kreutziger[1] has shown, celebrated secular agencies that became well known in urban centers, like Hull House, had their roots in Methodist urban missionary activities in the nineteenth century. Higher education was enhanced with the creation of colleges and universities. Theological education was awakened in part by a demand from laity for a cohort of preachers and pastors who were better prepared for ministries in a growing church. Finances, found to be insufficient for supporting the burgeoning systems of the denominational connection, were rebuilt around a new apportionment system.

One could look at Methodism's achievements in the later nineteenth and early twentieth centuries and conclude that, despite the disasters of internal division and external conflict, these were the most successful years in the life of the movement. Remarkably, the separations even seemed to promote new creativity. Within about a decade after the 1844 division, both northern and southern Methodists launched efforts to establish their own "national" churches in the country's growing capital city. When the trustees of Vanderbilt University successfully gained control of the institution, separating it from the authority of the church, Methodists in the South responded by creating two new schools, one west of the Mississippi (Southern Methodist University) and one east (Emory), and they are both still technically owned by the church.

Through nearly a century of separation, Methodism in the United States had to cope with some immensely difficult external circumstances that directly affected the internal life of the church. From the separation in 1844 to reunion in 1939, there was a steady stream of challenges that threatened to overwhelm the social order and the sacred life. Besides the Civil War, there were several economic disruptions, there were waves of immigration that brought large numbers of Roman Catholics to North America, and there were massive movements for social reform such as securing for women the right to vote. There was a World War, there was a Great Depression, there was racial hatred so deep that it led to lynchings, which were viewed as publicly entertaining spectacles in certain cities, there were disputes regarding the presence of Communists in the organized labor movement, there was distress over the violence generated by organized crime, and there was the specter of a Second World War on the horizon as the northern and southern and Protestant Methodists dramatically reunited in 1939.

Yet through all of that, in its fractured state, Methodism grew and prospered and made its public presence known across the face of North America. Perhaps breaking apart is not to be feared after all. At the very least, fractures are not fatal to the church.

Nevertheless, all fractures are painful. Many are terribly destructive. Most leave scars. Some are irreparable. None is eternal.

It would be inconsistent with the history of American Methodism to insist that the recovery of the church requires retaining the organizational entity called The United Methodist Church. It would also be inconsistent with the doctrinal history of Methodism to insist that for the sake of theological purity the denomination must divide. Neither schism nor the avoidance of schism will lead to the recovery of Methodism. The mere existence of an ecclesiastical institution accomplishes nothing. The readiness to sacrifice an ecclesiastical institution guarantees nothing.

For one of the things we should know, or may have to relearn in order to bring about the recovery of Methodism, is that the tradition does not claim any necessary or essential coherence between the institutional form of the church and its eternal promise.

My junior high school was in the coal-mining town of Glen Lyon, Pennsylvania. In the late nineteenth century and for the first half of the twentieth, it offered a place for hardworking miners and their families to have a decent life. Like many communities that existed in order to dig anthracite coal out of the earth and process it for home heating, it had drawn immigrants from eastern, central, and western Europe to the company-owned houses and stores along its streets—because mining coal and raising families in mining communities were the things those people knew how to do.

On its various streets were the churches where the miners and their families went to worship, where their children were baptized and married, where communities gathered for funerals. There were several Roman Catholic churches in Glen Lyon to care for the needs of different ethnic groups who expected to hear the Latin Mass in the accent of the old country, whatever that was. There were a very few scattered Protestant churches, all of which were tinier than the smallest of the Catholic parishes.

It was never an easy life for the miners or their families. The work was truly dangerous. The work schedule was unpredictable. Every day the afternoon newspaper published the mine schedule on its front page—which operations were "working" the next day, which ones would be "idle," and which ones were "undecided." To work was to face great risk. Not to work was to face hunger and hardship.

The community and the school and the churches and the mines were interlocked in many ways. In the 1950s, when I went to junior high in Glen Lyon, every school day began with prayer, which included a recitation of the Lord's Prayer. I learned early that I was part of a minority group—only a few of us Protestants uttered the lines of the prayer extolling God's "kingdom and the power and the glory forever." One day during the school hours, word spread that there had been a problem in one of the mines somewhere north of town. We prayed then too. Later we learned that miners had been removing coal from a column of rock beneath the river. Apparently too much rock had been removed, and the weight of the river crushed the pillars supporting the mine shaft. The river broke through the roof. Twelve miners were lost. One of them was the father of a friend in my junior high class.

None of us realized it at the time, but that day was more than a day that brought death into our junior high. It actually brought the end of underground anthracite coal mining in Glen Lyon and most surrounding communities. The river became a whirlpool that poured water into the mine shaft, and it continued for several days until the company found a way to stop the underground flood. By then it was too late. All of the mines in the area were filled with water. Twelve miners had died. And the coal industry was in the process of dying too.

A couple of decades later, I was back in Glen Lyon. My junior high days were a distant memory. My return to town was occasioned by my new responsibilities as a district superintendent in The United Methodist Church. Glen Lyon was within the bounds of my district.

Changes in the community were obvious. The big coal breaker that once spanned both sides of Main Street had been razed. A number of the Roman Catholic parishes had been merged, and some of their buildings were closed. Not only was it a community of declining population, it was in a diocese with a declining number of priests. The ethnic differences that once mattered a lot were no longer a priority. And, as far as I could tell, the only one of the Protestant churches remaining was a United Methodist congregation. It had only about six persons in attendance on an average Sunday, and it too should have been closed years earlier. It had continued to function because one man seemed to be a sufficient force with sufficient financial resources to keep it open. But his reasons were not a matter of Christian mission. He simply told me that he had been a member of that church all of his life, and his goal was to keep the building open until the day he died so that his funeral could be held there. After that, he said, he did not care what happened.

It is a painful thing to watch anyone die. Whether death comes to an individual, an institution, or a community, the demise is a tragedy. But there is something even more tragic about the sinful, selfish cynicism that seeks to keep an institution alive merely for the sake of personal gratification. My confession is that I failed to do anything about it during my term as a district superintendent.

The recovery of Methodism will not occur by the sheer effort to keep institutions open or to allow organizations without a mission to keep operating. One of the insidious aspects of the congregationalization of the church is the notion that congregations are to be sustained as institutions with the hope that they will find their way into mission. The truth is that a congregation of whatever size that is not mission-driven will never stumble into Christian mission.

Glen Lyon may be one of the smallest and saddest examples of what the recovery of Methodism cannot tolerate. But there are other examples.

First, there are churches—even thriving and growing ones—that use worship as a peculiar device for wooing people into the life of the congregation. That makes worship a marketing device for the church, not an act of praise to God. Some activities that pass for Sunday services are little more than entertainment for the body and the emotions rather than engagement with the mind and soul.

Several years ago, there was an observation made about a preacher whose Sunday services famously appeared on television—that it was hard to know whether he went on-screen to raise money or raised money so he could appear on-screen. Either way, the whole purpose of his services was to maintain a cycle of raising funds to telecast the services so he could raise funds to continue telecasting the services without end. But it was an entirely self-serving operation.

Methodism has its share of local churches that seem to use worship as a vehicle to draw a crowd and market the activities of the institution. Everything is then structured in ways to ensure that there will be a crowd—from parking lot ministries, to child care for the children of attendees, to amusing interludes within the service, to making sure that it ends in a timely manner. But those activities will not in themselves lead to the recovery of Methodism. They will only nourish the institutional maintenance of Methodism.

What we need are services like one I attended at a local United Methodist church some weeks ago in which the hospitality was so welcoming, the music was so energizing, the prayers were so fervent, and the preaching was so thoughtful that when the benediction came I looked at my watch and realized two hours had elapsed. It is not that services like that must take two hours. The same things could be celebrated in a single hour, for those congregations that have a schedule to keep. It's just that in truly great experiences of worship, time does not matter.

Second, for many in the church, mission has become monetized. That is, there are churches—including some institutionally successful ones—for whom mission is defined in terms of money. If the building is well maintained, if the staff are well compensated, if the apportionments are paid in full, and if benevolent giving continues to flow, then a congregation can tell itself that it is truly an effective church. But each of those measurements is monetary.

In the early years of the twentieth century, when Methodism's reliance on voluntary giving was not generating sufficient revenue to fund the missional initiatives and the institutional apparatus of the denomination, a new scheme was established to fund the connection's operations. Appreciation for the apportionment system suffered from the misfortune of being created by the church around the same time that the federal government created the income tax. Thus, by coincidence or not, Methodists habitually have considered apportionments as taxes levied on congregations.

The fact is that the apportionment system has generated significant revenues for some vital ministries. But it has also served to emphasize the problematic character of the congregationalization of the church. When the General Conference and the several annual conferences adopt their budgets, the revenue expectations are distributed through some formula by the General Conference to each annual conference and then by each annual conference to the local churches within its boundaries. Congregations and their pastors are then evaluated according to their performances on apportionments. It is not the only device to measure effectiveness, but it is a relatively simple one to monitor. Meanwhile, congregations and their pastors rarely participate in evaluations of the denominational agencies that spend those apportioned funds. So local churches can feel that they are expected to contribute financially to the larger mission of the denomination but not to participate in the mission of the denomination.

In a system that can assume participatory loyalty by the congregations of the denomination, and in an era where trust is high in those bureaucracies to carry out the will of the church effectively, that may be a viable mechanism. However, the twenty-first century is an age when brand-name identity may be high, but brand-name loyalty is not. A deep and broad level of trust cannot be assumed.

What has become clearly known about the rising generations of Americans is that they will support something financially if the mission is clear, if the cause is just, and if the communication is effective in demonstrating how the donor will be fulfilled as a person of faith by participating with a contribution. The apportionment system, however, is based upon institutional loyalty and organizational endurance. There is no evidence that those themes will sustain the church in the future.

The recovery of Methodism will require a new way to connect mission and money.

Third, there are churches that have lost track of the important connection between proclaiming the truth of the gospel and exercising the transforming power of the gospel. From its earliest days, Methodism defined its mission in terms of reforming the continent and spreading scriptural holiness over the land. Both of those are transformational goals. And both of those must be held together for the sake of the gospel.

What has happened, sadly, is that too many voices in the church have seen these goals as competitive rather than coordinating, common goals. Like the Wesleyan commitment to personal holiness and social holiness, these are inseparable. And yet, in a willingness to tolerate lesser dedication, adversarial forces in the church have chosen to tolerate a pursuit of one goal or the other, but not both. To stand in the public and proclaim, or to sit at a keyboard and write words—like the ones on the pages of this book—is a pointless and purposeless activity unless it is directed toward the goal of reforming the social order and promoting scriptural holiness.

On behalf of the church, there is no effective proclamation of the truth unless it brings about transformation. And there is no transformation unless it involves declaring the truth. What has happened within Methodism is that too many voices are talking only to the persons who already share their convictions. That makes them self-serving, if not entirely self-righteous crusaders. And it runs the risk of letting all of Methodism become what the Methodists in Glen Lyon had become in microcosm—an institution capable of enduring but without the capacity or commitment to transform the world.

The mission of the church is not fulfilled by the self-preservation of the church. God will sustain the church until the end of time. But its various institutional forms and congregations and bureaucracies and denominations have no everlasting merit. Only by finding and fulfilling the mission of the church will it endure.

The recovery of Methodism will require a willingness to receive that grace.

CHAPTER FIVE

Finding a Mission

"Love one another."
(John 13:34)

"Hold fast to the mystery of the faith with a clear conscience."
(1 Timothy 3:9)

Why would anyone want to become a Methodist—or a United Methodist—today? There are some parochial answers to that question. People are drawn to local churches in United Methodism for all sorts of reasons. One features a strong, vibrant youth ministry. Another has a music program of extraordinarily high quality. Another is vigorously active and well known in its community as an institution advocating the needs of an ethnic or racial or cultural minority. Another has a great preschool program for young children. Another has a senior minister whose sermons are compelling. Another has ample parking, with easy access exiting from and returning to a major highway. Another makes visitors feel especially welcome, with multiple greeters acknowledging their presence from the parking lot to the places they prefer to sit in the worship center. Another has the finest state-of-the-art facilities, with clean and inviting spaces that use the latest technological innovations. Another represents a strongly defined position on one or more political or doctrinal issues.

Many others use, or aspire to use, all of these effective devices aggressively for marketing their church. And they have developed more approaches to reach marginally interested or totally unchurched persons. Advertising campaigns by local churches have posted commercial billboards along the highways, have painted their names and logos on the exteriors of city buses, have bought advertising time on radio and television stations, have underwritten noncommercial programming on public radio and television outlets, have brought celebrities from the world of sports and entertainment to speak about topics other than faith at public events, have provided live-streaming or digitally recorded access to their pastors' sermons, and have conducted market analyses to determine whether and to what extent these ventures are effective.

For too long the church has failed to be market-wise. Many churches limited their outreach to purchasing a metal road sign from a religious supply house and hammering the sign into the ground at some prominent intersection. Years ago, one sociologist of religion commented that to be effective it is not the sign that should be placed in such a prominent location, it is the church building itself that should be constructed there! But most congregations followed a rather arrogant and foolish assumption that all one had to do was tell the public about a building in a reasonably visible place, post the times for worship, open the doors on Sunday, and the people would flock to the embrace of a pastor who was ready to shepherd them. But sheep generally do not hunt for a shepherd. They have to be sought and found. Nowadays, at least, there are many local churches that seem willing to use multiple marketing techniques in the search.

Yet it is one thing to be market-wise and another thing to be market-driven. To be market-wise is to recognize realities within which the church must learn to function. For example, years ago when I was pastoring a local church, I learned that planning a church program could predetermine the success or failure of an event based solely on the day and time it was scheduled. Adults who were middle-aged and older were less likely to attend a church event early on Sunday evening, for example, because network television programs tend to claim that demographic at that time. The best specific example is the CBS staple *60 Minutes*, which has dominated its time slot and has relied upon older adult reporters for decades. For similar marketing reasons, it is also clear that the most effective way to schedule Sunday mornings in a local church is to offer multiple worship opportunities at differing hours with overlapping Sunday school classes for children and adults. Some parents who have young children want to attend worship while the young ones are in class. Other parents want to attend worship with their children and, at another hour, separately attend adult classes while the children attend theirs. A market-wise church arranges its schedule to accommodate various preferences.

But a market-driven church is one that structures all of its ministries according to the shifting desires of potential constituencies. In a rush to satisfy urges for statistical improvements in membership and attendance, some local churches have decided to let the market—rather than the mission of Christianity—determine their ministries. Market-driven congregations, for instance, might decide to build massive parking garages to give attendees convenient, comfortable, close places to lock and leave their vehicles. Mission-driven congregations might spend the same dollars on building housing for the homeless people to live safely rather than housing for cars to be parked safely.

A church has to be sensitive to its market. But, in order truly to be a church, it has to be a servant of its mission.

Moreover, if—as in the case of Methodism—it is a connectional church rather than a congregational one, then the mission of the whole connection needs to be driving program priorities. All of these devices cited above for enticing or inviting people to become

United Methodists are local and congregational in character. They are means to recruit and retain persons for membership and involvement in particular local churches. They do not give the church a bigger profile in the nation or the world. They may help a specific local church to expand its presence in a particular community. But that is simply a matter of marketing one congregation in one marketable setting. It does not offer any incentive or motivation for a person to want to become a Methodist.

My maternal grandfather, on the other hand, was clear why he was a Methodist. He said it was the church that stood for the prohibition of beverage alcohol; or, to put it another way, Methodism was a temperance movement. Whether anyone today would want the denomination to reinstitute that specific missional priority is not the issue. The real point is that he shaped his spiritual life around an identifiable mission for which his own congregational affiliation was a local convenience. The mission of Methodism shaped the market for Methodism.

That particular theme was preeminent in his mind because, significantly, he had been raised in a home with an alcoholic father. He had witnessed the physical abuse and the economic deprivation visited upon himself and his siblings and their mother when too much alcohol took control of the household. But there were other aspects of Methodism's mission that led him to the denomination. For example, the Methodist Episcopal Church supported collective bargaining as one of the rights for the laboring classes. A unionized coal miner, he belonged to a church whose mission embraced him. His church supported his aspirations for justice, for workplace safety, and for personal rights. His local or regional relationship with a particular congregation was simply, in his view, an accident of where he happened to live. He identified his faith with Methodism as a mission and a movement—indeed, a movement for social transformation. He was not alone. As Michael Kazin has noted, "The Women's Christian Temperance Union supported trade unions, women's suffrage, and the municipal ownership of utilities."[1]

Frances Willard, among the most active Methodists and a leader of the WCTU, was a woman committed to a diverse agenda.

Methodism began as a renewal movement within an established church. That was its genesis and the start of its evolution. Recovering that capacity is Methodism's greatest opportunity. But to do so will require finding a mission.

It is certainly not the case that United Methodists lack a missionary impulse. The signs of engagement in mission activities abound.

To be sure, some of the historic mission-sending centers of service have waned. The United Methodist Women, whose lineage can be traced back more than a century and a half, has had many institutional forms including the Women's Foreign Missionary Society, the Women's Home Missionary Society, the Ladies' Aid Society, the Wesleyan Service Guild, and the Women's Society of Christian Service. Local units still generate and send to the Women's Division of the denomination's Board of Global Ministries substantial amounts of money for its mission programming. Yet, despite that long and distinguished history, the profile of the average women's unit now has a decidedly aging demographic. Except for a few rare situations, it has not found a way to appeal to the needs and interests of young professional women pursuing careers, or single women who are sole parents. Relative to funds that were raised in the past, current funding streams are shallower. And prospects are dim that they will improve.

Still, there are other active organized ventures making a difference in the life of the church for the transformation of the world. Volunteers in Mission span the continents and the globe through such projects as constructing schools, building clinics, and laying water supply systems. Habitat for Humanity initiatives build houses by the hundreds for prospective homeowners. Local church partnerships draw congregations together from different neighborhoods in the same city and from different nations across the seas. Strong congregations plant seeds for new local churches, often in neighborhoods that do not have the capacity to finance a new operation without help. Theological schools are preparing persons for ministry in a global context long before congregations invest themselves in a commitment to becoming or being a global church.

But all of those tend to be episodic and idiosyncratic programs, not a driving force or a passionate power that constitutes a common core of mission.

A novelist named Harold Frederic[2] wrote one of the great works of American fiction in the nineteenth century. *The Damnation of Theron Ware, or The Illumination* as he titled it, the book tells the story of a Methodist preacher in central New York State who experiences the disappointment of being sent to a lesser pastoral assignment than he felt his gifts deserved. From that opening and through a series of events as mundane as his effort to secure a salary increase and as bold as his decision to hire an itinerant evangelist, the novel describes the deterioration of his life and his ministry. In some respects, it illustrates what happens to leaders of the church who sacrifice their passionate dedication to mission by settling for a sequence of events that seems to offer satisfaction, pleasure, joy, or merely respite from the difficulties of the moment.

There is much about Methodism—especially about United Methodism—that has seemed to pursue such a course. "New ideas teach new duties," wrote James Russell Lowell, "time makes ancient good uncouth."[3] But some new ideas remain mere novelties unless they have broad institutional support, are based on a clear sense of mission, and generate durable commitments to provide resources for implementation. Bold ventures, such as the creation of Africa University and the National Plan for Hispanic Ministry, have been launched without any certainty that the church was ready or willing to provide the resources sufficient for turning the dreams of those programs into realities. Whether these efforts have merit is not in dispute. Whether they are linked to a shared sense of mission is, however, in doubt.

Lurching from one institutional venture to another occurs not only in programs but also in basic administration of the church.

Twice in the past quarter century (1980 and 2004), the denomination has revised its pension system. And then there is the matter of the restructuring of the church's ordained ministry. From the 1940s to the present, in every period except for two quadrennia, some committee or commission has been assigned to study the ordering of ministry in the denomination. In 1976, a concept of "representative ministry" was embraced and a form of lay leadership called "Diaconal Ministry" was created. Twenty years later the concept of representative was abandoned and the pattern of Diaconal Ministry was eliminated. Then newly constituted Orders of Deacon and Elder were established. Meanwhile, perhaps because of a meandering lack of clarity about the theology and structure of ordained ministry, there developed a lack of focus on what the church needs to require of its candidates preparing for the ordained ministry. Multiple educational pathways of preparation have been authorized, making no pretense of any consistency in the levels or areas of theological mastery that clergy can be assumed to have acquired.

Such shifting in programmatic, administrative, and ministerial aspects of church life suggests not so much a matter of sailing according to the winds of the Spirit as it does lurching across a sea of ideas in the hope of latching onto something that will actually work. It conveys the impression that we as a church do not know what we are doing, that we do not know what we want to do, that we do not know what we are being called to do. It is evidence of a church in need of theological and missional identity, a church hungering for spiritual power.

The recovery of Methodism requires that kind of power.

In the spring of 1988, I was a delegate to the General Conference of The United Methodist Church in St. Louis. On the Sunday that separated two hectic and demanding weeks of legislative business, a colleague and I went in search of a place to worship. We found our way to an African Methodist Episcopal Church. Uncertain of the travel time or the schedule of services, we arrived with nearly all hour to spare before worship began. So we explored the neighborhood a bit and wandered around the interior of the church building.

In the lower level we found a cozy room that served as a kind of museum for the history of the church. We learned that the congregation developed out of a preaching mission by Paul Quinn. In the middle of the nineteenth century, an African American like Quinn could live and preach freely in some places but not in others. Illinois was a free state. Missouri was a slave state. Quinn happened to be in Illinois. But he could not freely travel to the other side of the Mississippi River and enter Missouri. So he took a boat into the middle of the river and began preaching. Slaves on the Missouri side found their way to the riverbank, where Quinn's voice could reach them with the word. The fact that the law said he could not cross the river did not prevent the powerful mystery of the message from touching them. He proclaimed the gospel of deliverance and the church was born anew. The mission delivered the message across the river, across the boundary set by law and beyond the division separating slavery from freedom. And the people listened for that word.

The recovery of Methodism requires that kind of power.

I have been at a place of great power three times in my life. One is a place to which no reader of this book will ever be able to go. The second is a place that I hope few readers of this book will ever be forced to go, though some will. And the third is a place that perhaps at least a few readers of this book will be invited to go.

The first is a place that I visited with my father, just before he had to retire from his work as a plumber and pipe fitter because of ill health. He had emphysema, a lung disease that simply took his breath away. The last project on which he worked was a nuclear power plant. After the facility was built, but before it went into operation, each person who had worked on its construction was invited to bring a guest and take a guided tour of the entire site. My father invited me to be his guest. We examined the immense cooling towers, the huge steam turbines, the miles of piping, and then were allowed to move to the perimeter of the reactor core. We were told that, within a few weeks after our visit, the first of the fuel rods would be installed and the area would be sealed. Then the nuclear reaction would be started that would produce steam, that would turn turbines, that would generate electricity, that would power lights and appliances. But once that process started, the area would be a place of such power that no human being would be able to enter it for as long as 150,000 years. There is immense power in the world, but some of it cannot ever be touched. Inside that mighty space, no human voice will ever be heard again, but the mystery of the energy that binds the universe together will display its force every time a person touches a switch to turn on a light or to send an e-mail.

The second place of power that I have occupied was in a house that my wife and I owned when we lived in Durham, North Carolina. In 1996, a hurricane named Fran made landfall on the Carolina coast. We went to bed on a September night having heard the forecast that the storm would pass to the east and north of us, that we would experience some wind and rain, but that the damage in our immediate area would not be major since we would be on the western and weaker side of the storm. But the winds and the rain did not abate. To the contrary, they grew stronger. During the early morning hours, we could hear wind-driven rain pounding the exterior walls of the house as if bullets were being fired against it. And then, around 3:30 in the morning, the winds nearly ceased. The rain continued but sounded as if it were a fine spring mist gently showering the landscape. We had suddenly been shifted from an environment of noise and violence to an environment of remarkable stillness, serenity, and near silence.

In about forty-five minutes, the wind resumed—less violent than before and blowing from the other direction. That was when we realized that during those quiet minutes the eye of the storm had passed over us. The heart of the storm, its most powerful feature, had embraced our city, our neighborhood, our home. We learned that some of the most powerful forces in the world are the ones that arrive in silence and peace.

With the light of the morning, it was possible to see the damage that the storm had done. The wind and the rain had taken some lives during the night, had destroyed homes and businesses, and had inflicted much suffering. Yet, the greatest power that night was not in the noise like a roaring train or a barrage of bullets, but in the peace at the center of it all.

The third place of power that I have occupied was in Scranton, Pennsylvania, on a warm night more than three and a half decades ago. In the chronicles of human history it is a place that will generally go unnoticed and it was an event that few—even among the hundreds of persons who were present—will remember. I was kneeling at the altar in a United Methodist church building. The hands of a bishop were placed on my head. Then the arms and hands of an uncounted number of robed figures surrounded me, covered me, enclosed me as if I were in a tent. All the robes were black in those days, so the warm and humid place became a place of near total darkness. And in the midst of the darkness, the bishop spoke some words that announced I was being granted authority to administer the sacraments and to preach the word. The act of ordination, in what felt like a tent akin to the itinerant sanctuary that the people of the Old Testament carried with them in their wanderings, occurred in a place that was dark and damp and filled with the power of holy mystery.

Accordingly, the recovery of Methodism will require reconnecting to the sense that improving the mechanisms of the church will accomplish nothing unless the movement allows itself to be enfolded by the sacred mystery of God's presence. Part of that discovery involves appreciating that the most powerful places in the world are not the ones filled with noise but the ones that are silent. The cacophony of debate, the fury of argument, and the desire to determine whose votes sound the loudest when the "ayes" and the "nays" are counted do not exhibit sacred power. Real power is manifest when human voices grow quiet and when demands subside long enough to listen in sacred silence.

The recovery of Methodism will require finding a mission. And finding a mission will require more listening than talking. In the twenty-first century, what we may have to do is restore the discipline that lets us listen.

Several years ago, I traveled with a church group to England. Our purpose was to follow in the footsteps of John Wesley. And, under the leadership of some experienced guides, we visited all of the predictable spots as well as a few that were somewhat out of the way. We worshiped in the parish church at Epworth and received the sacrament of Holy Communion at the hands of the parish priest who used a paten and chalice dating from the eighteenth century, when the Reverend Samuel Wesley would have used them to offer the bread and the cup to his wife, Susannah, and their children. We went up to Oxford and looked into the colleges.

But we also visited a place in Cornwall called Gwennap Pit, where an old tin mine had collapsed into something that resembled a natural bowl. John Wesley used the Pit as an outdoor arena for preaching services. He discovered that its depressed terrain offered protection from the wind and that its bowl-like shape created some marvelous, natural acoustic qualities. He also claimed that it added immensely to the size of the crowd who could hear him, since the layers of the Pit could accommodate far more people than any flat open-air field would permit.[4] Then we tried an experiment. I stood on one terraced level a few steps below the top rim of the Pit. Our group of about thirty tourists gathered on the opposite side. I spoke in a normal, conversational tone and they heard every word without difficulty. But then something happened that Mr. Wesley would never have had to manage. An airplane approached, its jet engines loud enough even a few thousand feet in the air to prevent anyone in the Pit from hearing. In the twenty-first century, there is no doubt that the church's effort to listen has to cope with a lot more ambient noise.

But to find a mission will require us to listen. Amid the noise of some very angry debates, the church will have to listen to the silent pleas of immigrants who cross national boundaries with or without legal documents. Amid the sounds that emanate from many different kinds of music, the church will have to listen to the creative energies that quietly lie beneath the preferences of diverse cultures and generations. Amid the roaring cries that respond to whatever is entertaining, whatever holds the status of celebrity, whatever insists that happiness will come only if we purchase this product, the church will have to find the silence in the spaces that lie between noises. For that is where the mystery and the power and the glory of God will help the church find its mission again.

One way to achieve that is to reestablish the practices of prayer. I refer here not to communal acts of prayer that involve reading printed texts aloud, though that is a tremendously important aspect of spiritual life. Nor am I referring to the routine acts of reciting learned prayers as if the objective work of repeating familiar syllables will renew the faith, though the regular recitation of others' prayers (like the one from Saint Francis of Assisi or the "serenity" prayer of Reinhold Niebuhr) can be helpful steps in maintaining the discipline of prayer. I refer to finding a space for recovering the practice of silence.

On a spring day in the 1990s, the commencement speaker at a university in North Carolina was the late Fred Rogers—Mr. Rogers to generations of American families. A Presbyterian with a theological education, he had been requested by the graduates in the class partly because he represented the one cultural experience that nearly all of these young adults had in common. He began his speech in a manner that was not terribly unusual, suggesting that the graduates take a minute to think about all of the people who had assisted them in their educational and personal journeys, who had sacrificed in ways that made a college education possible, who had encouraged them at difficult times in their lives. And then, having asked the graduates to take a minute for this exercise, he stopped talking, looked down at his watch, and let the sixty seconds of the minute pass. Apparently at the start of this exercise in silence, some of the

graduates had difficulty becoming quiet. Then silence settled over the stadium. Then the sounds of individuals' struggling to cope with tears could be heard. After a minute, Fred Rogers began to speak. But the opportunity to listen to their own thoughts and memories and souls was a greater gift for many of these graduates than anything else they received that day. For some, in fact, it was the first time they had ever heard the beauty of silence.

Methodists have for too long practiced effectively the art of noise. We sing. We argue. We talk during frequent fellowship meals. But even when we could practice the disciplines of silence, we often choose not to do so. Worshipers who come forward for Holy Communion in many local churches do so with congregational or choral singing filling the air. Organ voluntaries at the opening and closing of many traditional services are used as times to move about, to chat about the previous day's game, or to discuss the plans for a meal afterward. Electronic music during so-called contemporary services gives a vibrant feel to the experience but can impose itself so strongly that it stifles the freedom to feel an unheard power.

Finding a mission will require listening more than speaking. It will require attending to the spaces between the words of discussion and debate more than to the words of discussion and debate themselves.

There is a story about the veteran preacher who heard a young minister preach on the text from Micah that we must do justly, love mercy, and walk humbly with God. The elder commended the younger for the effort, but then added that anybody can preach on those three phrases rather effectively. The challenge, said the senior preacher, is whether you can preach on the commas. Sometimes the most powerful word is the one embedded in the pauses between the words and in the silences that separate what is spoken.

Those are the places for the practice of prayer. And the recovery of Methodism will require that, for it is the means of access to spiritual power.

CHAPTER SIX

American Methodism and Methodism of Americans

"Give therefore to the emperor the things that are the emperor's, and to God the things that are God's."

(Matthew 22:21)

S everal decades ago, Bishop Gerald Kennedy published a volume called *The Methodist Way of Life*.[1] Around the same time, in a three-volume set covering the history of American Methodism, Bishop F. Gerald Ensley published a chapter that described The Methodist Church as the most American of denominations.[2] Looking back on that era, it hardly seems that there really was a possibility one could imagine a way of life that was distinctly Methodist in North America or that a denomination would feel uncritically good about being Americanized.

Yet there has been a feeling broadly held among many Methodists in the United States that it is neither useful nor necessary to separate the American way of life from the Methodist way of life—whatever those phrases may mean. To put the matter in its most pedestrian and broadest form, Methodists in the United States generally have not drawn a bright line between allegiance to Christianity and allegiance to the country.

To be sure, there certainly are voices that claim it is, or wish it were, otherwise. Nevertheless, Methodism in the United States has not defined itself as a sect over against the prevailing national culture. Some Methodists have taken conscientious positions in opposition to war. Yet plenty of Methodist churches posted signs or plaques within their buildings during the 1940s with the names of their members who served in the uniform of the United States military during World War II, honoring service to the country during the war. And, of those churches who did so, most had a gold star by at least a few of those names, identifying the soldiers or sailors or airmen who were killed in action or later died of war wounds. Prayers for peace by Methodists have been regularly offered, but they have never established an agenda that allowed the denomination to be labeled a "peace church."

There have been a few Methodist churches that engaged in vigorous debate about the question of whether to display the American flag in the sanctuary, but a large majority of Methodist congregations would not even entertain such a discussion. They assume the flag of the nation belongs there. If the matter were to be debated at all, the only question would concern whether the flag should be on the right or the left of the pulpit!

On a more subtle level, there has also been an alliance between the interests of the Methodist people and the issues of interest to the United States. Intense debates erupt in the General Conference of The United Methodist Church about the language of the Social Principles embraced by the denomination. Yet most of the matters addressed are related to the concerns of North American Christians. Efforts to have the church identify itself as a global community have not prevented the Social Principles from being phrased in ways that display the hegemony of Methodists in the United States. Topics including abortion, homosexuality, capital punishment, and gun control are rarely going to evoke the same kind of intense disagreement in some Asian, African, and Latin American Methodist contexts as they evoke in North America.

A second underappreciated subtlety is the comfortable connection between the Methodist system and the economic system in the United States. There are several aspects of this, beginning with the way that taxes of various kinds are structured. United Methodists today rely upon the acceptance of property tax exemptions for the church's religious, educational, and social institutions. Many pay fees in lieu of taxes to local municipalities and states as a way of contributing to the costs of basic services including police presence, fire control, and emergency assistance. All try to make maximum use of the sales tax exemptions that states permit religious organizations to enjoy. And the gifts contributed by members and friends of the church are actively promoted for the personal benefit of tax deductibility that donors value. These elements are rather modest compared to the immense importance that Methodism places on the American economic system for the care of its own clergy and lay staff. The denomination's pension program encourages confidence in corporate stock funds, mutual funds, commercial bond funds, and other instruments of investment. Clergy are more likely to maintain a regular watch on their retirement portfolios than on the emerging scholarly perspectives on the Synoptic Gospels.

Over the years there have certainly been a few prominent Methodists who have held anticapitalist views. Harry F. Ward may have been one of the most notorious. To varying degrees, William Jennings Bryan supported some items that were important to socialists, and Frances Willard was a Christian Socialist.[3] But Methodism remained within the broad middle of economic life in the United States and did not issue any call for political or economic revolution.

There is another way that American Methodism exhibited the North American mind-set of the United States, and that is evident in the aspects of global mission work that seemed to export not only the Christian faith but also the cultural patterns of life with colonialist attitudes. Bringing the faith to another culture often meant replicating the North American culture along the way. United

Methodists from Zimbabwe, for example, can recall the early missionaries trying to eliminate indigenous patterns of African music from worship and substituting instead the hymnody that was familiar to North American and European patterns of praise. In Mexico City today there are two sizable and active Methodist congregations, one of which traces its founding to the work of missionaries from the Methodist Episcopal Church, South, and the other to the Methodist Episcopal Church in the northern United States.

But the strongest pieces of evidence that the Methodist way of life sought to link itself with the American way of life exist within the United States. Many church bodies set their boundaries in conformity with those of the respective nations in which they are located. The Episcopal Church, for instance, fashions ties to the Anglican Communion in the rest of the world by linking national churches to the Archbishop of Canterbury. In its own way, perhaps, Methodism in the United States was seeking to become an American church.

Institutions of National Identity?

First, there are institutions that Methodism created to embody this relationship. In the 1850s, shortly after the denomination divided over the issues of slavery and related matters, both the Methodist Episcopal Church and the Methodist Episcopal Church, South, took action to establish their own "national churches" as congregations in the nation's capital.

The General Conference of the northern church acted in 1852 to create its national church. The Reverend Henry Slicer was named the first pastor—actually calling him its "agent"—to travel the country and raise funds for the construction of a building that would meet the needs of Methodism in the country's capital city. The project was interrupted by the Civil War and then restarted, with the new building finished and dedicated in February 1869. The chair of the Board of Trustees who acted on behalf of the congregation as its official leader in the dedication ceremonies was Ulysses S. Grant, who was to be inaugurated five days later as president of the United States.

Grant was the first of several presidents with ties to the national church. Another was William McKinley, a member of the congregation. When McKinley was shot and lingered near death for many days before succumbing to his wounds, the Methodist president was credited with showing the nation how a person of faith—to be more precise, how a Methodist—faced death and forgave his attacker. McKinley was not the only Methodist on the national political scene, for his sometime political adversary William Jennings Bryan was another. But through the tragedy of the assassination attempt that eventually claimed his life, McKinley became the most dramatic and visible example to the nation of how such a person of faith might face the ultimate challenge. His funeral in the sanctuary of the national church near the White House further reinforced that point.

Soon after the decision of northern Methodism was made known, the Methodist Episcopal Church, South, established Mount Vernon Place Methodist Church as "the South's representative church" to be the national voice of southern Methodism in Washington. The church began to function in 1856.

Three decades later, Methodism decided to add a university of the denomination in the nation's capital. Interestingly, it was not called Methodist University but rather the "American University." And three decades after that, around the time that the Methodist Building was being constructed on Capitol Hill adjacent to the Supreme Court Building on one side and the United States Capitol on the other, an idea was advanced to build an additional structure in the Wesley Heights neighborhood of Washington, D.C., across from the American University to the north and a new building to be constructed for Metropolitan Memorial Church, the National Methodist Church, to the east. Had that plan come to fruition, Methodism would have housed all of its denominational agencies, its American University, and its national church on adjacent campuses on one of the highest points of land in the city.

The idea seemed to symbolize the hope that Methodism and the United States would have, in the capital of the country, a common institutional center. Simply that such a vision could be nurtured is the first item of evidence that Methodism wished to be identified with the nation.

Constitutional Consistency?

A second bit of evidence about the linkage between American Methodism and the American way of life is the suggestion of a constitutional consistency between the two. This may be more apparent than it is real. A casual observer will see that there are three branches of constitutional government in the United States—executive, legislative, and judicial—and that there appear to be three similar branches of constitutional governance in United Methodism—bishops, General Conference, and Judicial Council. From time to time one will hear the Judicial Council of The United Methodist Church described as the denomination's "supreme court." And some observers see the bishops as the executives who must carry out the laws of the church, with the General Conference being the body that writes the laws.

But actually the polity of the church is much more complex than that. It is true that the General Conference has legislative responsibility for all things that are distinctly connectional. And it is true that the Council of Bishops exercises spiritual and temporal oversight of all matters for the church. And it is also true that the Judicial Council has authority to decide whether some laws of the church are constitutional within the church. Nevertheless, when the General Conference passes a law that specifies no self-avowed, practicing homosexual may be ordained or appointed to a place of ministry, it is not only (or even mainly) a bishop who administers that law—it is actually the clergy members of each annual conference who do so.

It may be that somewhere in the vision of American Methodism there was a glimmer of an idea that the church and the nation would have systems of governance akin to each other. If so, it has not actually happened that way. One of the ways that United Methodism remains truly distinctive in its life and official administration is the nature of its connectional constitution. A system of interlocking conferences actually administers the policies and the legislative acts of the denomination. It gives the church a kind of flexibility and freedom that maintains ecclesial identity apart from any national identity.

A Common Chronology?

Third, there is the fact of a common chronology. Methodism arrived in North America as part of the colonial move from England. John Wesley lists his experience in Georgia as one of the three rises of Methodism, and he came to Georgia as part of the effort to found a colony under the leadership of General Oglethorpe. Wesley was the chaplain. Though he ran afoul of the law, faced a bill of indictment, and felt forced to flee back to England, he was personally part of the colonial enterprise. Moreover, his Tory sympathies led him to view the colonists' desire for independence from the Crown as a truly strange notion. Yet the outcome of the Revolutionary War, coupled with his own advanced age, left him little choice but to find a means to honor the independence of Methodism in America from his control in England.

A common chronology of church history and political history therefore links the Methodist experience and the American experience in the United States. Independence was declared in 1776 and claimed at the end of the Revolutionary War in 1783. Wesley authorized the Methodist Episcopal Church in the United States to be established as an independent entity in 1784. Twenty years after a Constitution for the United States was adopted, a constitution for The Methodist Episcopal Church was adopted. When states seceded from the United States to form the Confederacy, launching the Civil War, the boundaries of the Confederate States of America were roughly the same as those of the Methodist Episcopal Church,

South, which had become separate from Methodism in the North about seventeen years earlier.

The politics of race were displayed similarly in the church and in the society, with legislated segregation creating separate and unequal systems in the church and in the nation. Methodism's Central Jurisdiction was established in 1939, for instance, to ensure that the races would remain separate. But even where such official matters as salaries and expense accounts for the bishops in all jurisdictions were established as equal, there were clear inequities. The bishops of the Central Jurisdiction had to travel far greater distances than the bishops of the five regional jurisdictions to fulfill their responsibilities to churches and conferences, for their pastoral charges, districts, and annual conferences were spread across the country, not limited to a geographic section of the continent.

It was only when the remaining egregious laws establishing segregation were overcome in the 1960s that Methodism managed to dismantle its own apartheid system. In fact, it was not until the year of Martin Luther King Jr.'s assassination, in 1968, that the Central Jurisdiction was finally eliminated.

The common chronology of the United States and The Methodist Church was not limited to political history or racial separation. It was demonstrated in gender bias as well. Women were granted full clergy rights by The Methodist Church in 1956. But the actual entrance into and enjoyment of those rights in any substantial numbers did not occur for women until at least two more decades had passed. As a practical matter, that meant it was a long time after the formal approval was granted before women received master's degrees from theological schools, were approved by the clergy of annual conferences for ordination, and were appointed as pastors of local churches. In fact, these achievements occurred generally around the same time as—or a little later than—any notable number of women began to emerge from law school and pass the bar, or graduate from medical school and become practicing physicians. At best the church was a mirror of American society on the acceptance of women in professional leadership, not a leader within the society.

Even now, there remain many unknowns. How many women, at some early stage of pursuing candidacy in the complex United Methodist process toward ordination, have been discouraged by some committee or board in the system? How many have simply decided to sacrifice any hope of being ordained? How many of those who have been ordained have reached the stained-glass ceiling, which seems to be inhibiting the appointments of women to the most significant places of leadership as senior pastors of large membership churches?

Embedded in the American way of life and in the patterns of gender limitation that are so common in the American way of life, Methodism has not demonstrated a capacity or courageous willingness to be a pioneer in establishing women in leadership. Instead, the church has followed other professions and let medicine and law take the lead. Clergywomen constitute a lower percentage of the delegates to the General Conference than nonordained women constitute among the lay delegates.

The recovery of Methodism will be restrained by this pattern of continuing to keep women in reduced numbers among church leaders. It is not, in this case or any other, some principle of numerical balance that must be achieved. It is, rather, the case that the mission of the church requires a celebration of the biblical principle that there is "neither male nor female" in the community of the gospel.

The sad fact is, on issues of both race and gender, Methodism has not felt missionally compelled to reform the continent or spread scriptural holiness over the land. Notwithstanding its mission to transform society, the movement has merely conformed to social patterns.

In the early years of the twenty-first century, there are signs that the same thing is occurring in matters of ethnic bias against Latino and Latina immigrants. In the eastern Pennsylvania city of Hazleton and in the north Texas community of Farmers Branch, a pattern has begun to be established that finds ways to identify

Hispanic persons and create legal devices for driving them out of their homes, their workplaces, and their well-being. The shibboleth that only "illegal" persons are the targets of investigations or raids does not acquire merit simply by being endlessly repeated. It was illegal for certain persons to drink from some water fountains fifty years ago, too.

Is it the role of the church to affirm the established pattern in a country and thus conform to the existing law? Or is it the role of the church to listen to the Spirit of God, to hear the call beckoning it to fulfill its mission, and to transform both social order and personal discipline?

In one of my academic assignments, I was scheduled to attend a conference in Fayetteville, North Carolina. Having never been to the city, I asked for a set of driving directions and took the recommended exit from the highway. That's when my generally bad sense of direction and my penchant for becoming disoriented in an unfamiliar place took control. Within about ten minutes, I knew that I was confused to the point of being lost.

Fortunately, I saw a motel connected to one of the major national chains and decided to ask for directions to my destination. The woman at the desk was very patient and very accommodating. She gave me a simple set of traffic lights to count and turns to make. "Then," she said, "you will go around the marketplace and you will find the site of your conference on your right." Because she had been so helpful and because she had actual paying customers waiting for me to leave, I did not want to ask anything further from her. Her reference to the "marketplace" had not exactly been clear, but I decided I would be able to recognize a shopping mall when I came upon it.

But the marketplace in Fayetteville is not a place to go shopping. Or at least it is not a place to go shopping now. It used to be a place to buy slaves. The brick-and-stone structure, complete with shackles and an auction block, has remained in the center of the city as a sign of what once was permissible and perfectly legal. Would the auction block have been turned sooner into an artifact of the past if

Methodism had embraced its mission, reforming at least part of the continent and spreading scriptural holiness over the land?

To be sure, in some places voices were raised. Most dramatic was William Wilberforce, who, on May 12, 1789, spoke to the British House of Commons for four hours about the evils of the slave trade. He knew that he was challenging a legal and lucrative activity that in one year alone had added seventeen million pounds to the economy in the city of Liverpool. He knew that detail, and plenty of others, because he had spent two years studying the matter before he uttered a word about it in the House of Commons. He also knew that no single speech, even one of immense length such as his marathon, would be enough to turn the tide. Indeed, it took eighteen years from the date of his speech for Parliament to abolish the slave trade in Britain. And he knew as well that no speech, if it merely excoriated his adversaries for their misdeeds, would transform the society or the individuals whom he was addressing. So he included himself in the ranks of those who needed redemption. "I mean not to accuse anyone," Wilberforce said, "but to take the shame upon myself, in common with the whole parliament of Great Britain, for having suffered this horrid trade to be carried on under their authority. We are all guilty, we ought all to plead guilty, and not to exculpate ourselves by throwing the blame on others."[4]

Two years after Wilberforce delivered this speech, John Wesley died. But before his death, Wesley joined in affirming the message and bade his church to do the same. Not all Methodists did. Perhaps with the failure to honor the mission of the church and do so, the fracturing of Methodism in America became not only inevitable but necessary.

Other voices in other eras have summoned the church to hear a similar word. In the early 1960s, when discord over school desegregation was dividing Methodists into various factions across the country, especially in the South, twenty-eight Methodist preachers in Mississippi prepared a statement that was published in the *Mississippi Methodist Advocate*.[5] Titled "Born of Conviction," the statement affirmed freedom of the pulpit, the unity of all races, and the preservation of public school education. It expressed the view of the twenty-eight signers that they were "unalterably opposed to the closing of public schools" and to the use of public funds for segregated, private schools. Finally, the statement declared that Christ "defends the underprivileged, oppressed, and forsaken" and "challenges the status quo." Most of the signers were younger ministers, among them Jim Waits, who later became dean at Candler School of Theology, and Maxie Dunnam, who later became president of Asbury Seminary. All but nine of the twenty-eight left the Mississippi Conference, and a number of them left the ministry.

The fulfillment of the mission of Methodism in America requires a prophetic and transforming word, not simply a conforming mindset. But meeting this requirement is not without its costs.

Methodism faces a huge risk in the early decades of the twenty-first century. For most of the past hundred years, there has been an increasing trend toward congregationalizing the church. Strong affinities with American culture can insidiously reinforce that trend, for independent congregations have tended to be seen as the norm in most religious organizations. This direction alone could further deprive Methodism of its identity as a connectional movement, making it more comfortable with a conforming approach to ministry than a transforming approach to ministry. In turn, that would lead to further separation from the mission of the church, to reform the continent and spread scriptural holiness over the land.

The polity of the connectional church and the prophetic capacity of the church allow Methodism—including United Methodism—to secure its freedom while remaining institutionally incarnate within the American way of life. Methodism is not a sectarian body that seeks to separate itself from the larger culture, nor is it captive to the systems and instruments of any particular national culture.

The recovery of Methodism will require a recognition and celebration of that truly distinctive place on the religious landscape of the nation and of the nations.

CHAPTER SEVEN

Oversight and Accountability

"Respect those who labor among you,
and have charge of you in the Lord and admonish you."
(1 Thessalonians 5:12)

One of my mentors in the early years of ministry offered a number of maxims that he thought would assist me toward greater effectiveness. Among them was his advice about the importance of making the right judgments. He said, "There are many things you will have to oversee. It is even more necessary to develop discernment about what not to overlook."

The task of oversight is entrusted to a variety of persons in Methodism. Laity hold vital volunteer responsibilities as the elected officers, stewards, chairs, presidents, and other positions of leadership. Clergy are accountable for the ministries entrusted to their care in local pastorates, institutional chaplaincies, academic professorships, and the discipline of their clergy colleagues. Laity and clergy hold professional staff positions in denominational agencies, faith-based community organizations, and local churches. Every one of these persons is accountable in many ways for overseeing programs and personnel. Every one of them is also accountable for making discerning judgments about what not to overlook.

The terribly tragic circumstances that have come to light in recent years involving the sexual abuse of children by Roman Catholic priests has made known the even more tragic failures of church leaders, including bishops, to exercise appropriate leadership. In overseeing the life of the church, there have been too many cases where bishops chose to overlook the hurt and the harm that were being inflicted and the crimes that were being committed. In Methodist circles, almost anyone who has been a bishop or a district superintendent knows some secrets about financial or sexual misconduct by one or more among the members of the clergy, when the problems were handled by quick and quiet changes of appointment, often to some less desirable location as a punitive act. That approach has been used under the rubric of overseeing the church, but in fact it may have amounted to overlooking something harmful in the life of the church.

How does one know what to oversee and what not to overlook in being faithful and accountable?

One bit of lore known to almost every former and current district superintendent concerns the practical professional preparation for the office. Bishops, in consulting with individuals about accepting an appointment to the cabinet, have often been asked, "How will I know the content of the job description for this position?" Their customary answer is, "You will know when you receive your first phone call."

When I heard that from a bishop, I thought it was a comical cliché, until—four weeks into my appointment as a district superintendent—I received a call from one of the pastors in the district. He said he was coming to see me and he was bringing a friend. It was the first step in a sequence of events that led to his announcement that he was "a gay man without the gift of celibacy." That's when I knew that the superintendency would be a continuing and challenging act of discernment and discipline on some exceedingly hard issues. One phone call was enough to help me understand the job description.

During my ensuing years in office, I realized that many phone calls would come from persons who were very angry. There was the man who called and was irate that his church's pastor was engaged in a sexual affair with his wife. There was a pastor who called and was extremely angry that his local church committee on finance rejected the recommendation of the pastor-parish relations committee that he get a raise. There was the chair of a pastor-parish relations committee who called and was angry that I had made a decision to move her beloved pastor to a different church—apparently not knowing that the pastor had explicitly told me that she wanted to move elsewhere.

Then there was the day that an angry pastor called me about an administrative crisis involving church property. He told me that some basic repairs needed to be made in the parsonage and that he had been pressing the Board of Trustees to take care of the items. The previous month, at a board meeting, they had voted to do so. About two weeks after that meeting of the trustees, having heard nothing about any specific plans or schedule for the work to be done, the pastor contacted the chair of the board and asked about the arrangements for the work. "Oh," said the chair, "we decided not to do that."

Apparently, following the adjournment of the meeting when the board voted to proceed with the repairs, a few members of the board gathered around their cars in the church parking lot. They chatted about various matters and reached a consensus that the work in the parsonage did not really need to be done.

The pastor was furious and frustrated. He asked me, "What are you going to do about it?" He was assuming, not incorrectly, that I had some responsibility for oversight of the church property of the district. I asked for a little time to ponder the matter. He was still angry. But he conceded that I could have some time, which I used to develop a list of accountability options.

One is that the trustees in a congregation have legal and fiduciary responsibility for the assets of the local church, including the care of the real estate that the church owns. Simply put, in the case of this specific local church, that means the Board of Trustees has oversight of the church building and of the parsonage. Therefore, oversight and accountability rest with the Board of Trustees for the condition of the parsonage, for finding the funds to make any needed repairs, for hiring appropriate contractors to do the work, for recruiting volunteers to handle the work, or for deciding to do nothing and let the building deteriorate.

A second is that every annual conference sets some parsonage standards that it considers the minimum for each appointment in the conference. Typically these include specifying the number of bedrooms, the types of appliances, the presence of a study (in lieu of or in addition to an office at the church), the provisions for lawn care, the utility or other connections for telecommunications, and possibly many more items. The bishop of each annual conference has responsibility for the spiritual and temporal affairs of the church. One can argue that the parsonage standards within the annual conference belong under the heading of temporal affairs, so the bishop bears responsibility for seeing that those standards are met in every case. Therefore, the bishop could determine that the local church Board of Trustees will either maintain the parsonage in accordance with the annual conference standards, or the pastor will be housed elsewhere at local church expense.

A third is basically the same as the second, except that the bishop views the office of district superintendent as an extension of the office of the bishop. The bishop delegates to the superintendent the authority to tell the Board of Trustees that either they must meet the minimum parsonage standards or they must pay for the pastor and the pastor's family to be housed elsewhere.

A fourth is that the angry pastor could put the whole matter into the hands of the civil courts. The pastor could sue the local church Board of Trustees for dereliction of duty in caring for the parsonage. The pastor could also sue the superintendent and the bishop for failing to exercise their responsibilities as overseers of the temporal affairs of the church, specifically with regard to the parsonage. The pastor could sue everyone (the Board of Trustees, the bishop, and the superintendent) for the pain and suffering that this whole episode has caused him and his family. Such suits would seek to trust the county court to adjudicate the whole matter. If the court were to agree to hear the case or cases, then it would be up to the court to determine where the pastor would live and under what conditions.

A fifth is that the district superintendent could convene a special session of the charge conference, or a special session of a church conference, or a special session of a church local conference, to address the issue. In this procedure, the superintendent would exercise oversight and accountability by using the authority to convene a meeting and let the laity of the local church resolve the matter by going around the Board of Trustees, if necessary.

A sixth is that the bishop and all of the district superintendents collectively, as the cabinet, could declare that the housing conditions in this setting are not suitable for the assignment of any pastor. Then the bishop could announce that this pastor is being moved to a different appointment and that no other pastor will be appointed to this church until the housing situation is settled. Quite possibly this approach could provoke some legal challenge from one or more sources. The church that is, in effect, being deprived of a pastor may assert that the bishop and the superintendents have breached their contract to appoint a pastor to their community. Moreover, some other local churches might begin to wonder whether this is simply a power grab by the bishop and could entertain some sort of civil court action—or file grievances against the bishop and the superintendents that might lead to ecclesiastical court action.

A seventh is that the annual conference could decide that the trustees' neglect of the property was tantamount to abandoning it. Then the conference could take control of the parsonage by exercising the trust clause in the United Methodist *Discipline* that clearly states local churches own property in trust for the denomination as a whole and that, should the property be abandoned, it reverts to the annual conference.

An eighth is that the district superintendent could file a complaint against the pastor for incompetent administration of the ministerial office. That could lead to a temporary removal of the pastor from the situation until the charges were adjudicated according to the procedures outlined in the *Discipline*. Eventually, the clergy members of the annual conference would have to process the charges, and they could eventually lead to a church trial. In this approach, oversight and accountability would begin with the cabinet in evaluating whether the clergy are faithfully exercising their administration of the pastoral office. In the end, oversight and accountability for determining whether the pastor is faithfully fulfilling the responsibilities of the pastoral office would rest with the clergy of the annual conference.

None of these options is exclusive of any other possibilities on the list. All of these options collectively do not exhaust the possible ways to manage the crisis at hand. In essence, when it comes to handling an issue raised by an angry pastor or a layperson, Methodism has many different ways for defining oversight that can appropriately be exercised and accountability that can be assigned in a matter of managing ministry. A part of discernment is simply deciding which instrument among the many to use.

But that is a property matter. What options does Methodism have for dealing with the extremely serious problems facing its mission? Who will exercise oversight and accountability for finding the mission of the church?

A perfectly legitimate answer to that question is "All of the above." Clergy, laity, superintendents, and bishops all have that responsibility and are accountable for fulfilling some role in oversight.

Unfortunately, that answer is both correct and useless. It is indeed correct that everybody—the clergy and the laity, the bishops and the superintendents, the members and staff of the local churches and the members and staff of the annual conferences, the executives and support staff of general agencies and the faculty and staff of church-related institutions—has some role in oversight and accountability for identifying and articulating the mission of the church. But it is also useless to assert that, because the result would simply be a cacophony of voices, both official and unofficial, claiming to offer the authentic and authoritative statement of the church's mission.

The situation with the local church pastor, whose parsonage repairs continued to suffer from neglect, demonstrated that United Methodist polity is so inconclusively and imprecisely constructed that it does not offer a single unified method for handling what is actually a trivial dispute. It permits many options. But it is not at all clear that United Methodism offers any options for resolving a truly serious theological challenge.

In basic terms, the church appears to have no office or committee or council capable of finding its lost mission. There is no single spot within the denominational bureaucracy conducting such a search. And yet, as the situation regarding repairs for the parsonage demonstrated, this is a church whose polity appreciates and respects the complexities of the world.

Given that, we might say that Methodism actually is better suited than most ecclesiastical bodies to finding a means for its own recovery. For it has the capacity to respond patiently and creatively to a diverse array of challenges. The response, however, may involve its own set of complexities.

The Ecclesiastical Dance

First, there is the intricate balance among legislative, executive, and judicial authority that is distributed across so many conferences and councils of the church. When that arrangement works well, it can look like a superbly collegial interaction or even a gracious dance with partners collaborating beautifully together. On occasion, that balance topples over into chaos and conflict. What contributed to the separation of northern and southern Methodism in 1844, besides the intractable dispute over slavery, was an equally problematic inability to resolve conflicting interpretations of the relationship between the bishops and the General Conference. Could the conference exercise legislative authority over the separate and self-governing body of bishops? The church split and the matter was left unsettled.

In United Methodism today, the General Conference has complete authority to write the laws of the denomination, and it has the ability to create agencies whose duties are to administer the matters that have been written into church law. But neither the General Conference nor any of its agencies has authority to enforce these ecclesiastical laws. Some laws may be enforced by a bishop, and some can be enforced only by the clergy members of an annual conference. For instance, bishops are granted by church law the power to deprive an ordained person of the right to exercise the ministerial office temporarily—if that person is accused of some serious ecclesiastical offense. But the power is only temporary.

The real authority to remove someone from the ordained ministry lies with the annual conference in which an individual holds clergy membership. And the authority to decide who meets the legislative requirements for ordination that have been set by the General Conference rests with the clergy members of each annual conference. Thus, the Northwest Texas Annual Conference may reject an individual candidate for ordination on the grounds that the specific individual has been identified as a self-avowed, practicing homosexual. And no matter what the bishop of that conference may think, it is not the bishop's prerogative to proceed with an ordination if the annual conference clergy have refused to approve it. However, the California-Nevada Conference may look at an identical dossier from a candidate and vote to approve the person for ordination. And no matter what the bishop of that conference may think, it is not the bishop's prerogative to refuse ordination if the annual conference clergy have voted to grant it. Accountability for enforcing the laws written by the General Conference rests in these matters with the clergy members of each annual conference.

As Bishop James K. Mathews has written, the bishops' control of church affairs "is mostly moral and becomes evident in authenticity more than in power and authority as such."[1] Bishops ordain, but they do not decide whom to ordain. Bishops may file official complaints charging misconduct by clergy. But if their complaints are not sustained by the members of the annual conference, they cannot refuse to appoint the clergy whose conduct they found so offensive and objectionable.

The situation is even more delicate with regard to money than it is with regard to ministry. The General Conference adopts a four-year budget for the denomination as a whole. It then allocates the revenue requirements of that budget to the annual conferences in the United States and expects them to pay it. The annual conferences devise formulas for allocating their portions of the general budget to local churches and expect them to pay it. But there are almost no mechanisms available for enforcing any element or layer of these allocations. And the ones that are available, such as punitively moving a pastor to a less lucrative appointment or garnishing the pension of a pastor whose church fails to pay its apportionments, are rarely used. Payment of the apportionments is almost entirely voluntary by the local churches. To have a balanced budget requires a balance among the parts of the connection. In Methodism's ecclesiastical dance, accountability is a shared responsibility.

Tangled Practices

Second, while attempting to maintain the balance and to continue the dance, some operational and functional decisions have been made that create additional confusion. It is the standard operating procedure for the Council of Bishops of United Methodism to assign one or more of their number to each of the governing boards of the agencies that the General Conference has created. It has become customary that, when the governing boards of these agencies meet to elect officers, a bishop is elected to the presidency of the board.

Such a practice shifts the role of the bishop from episcopal oversight of the work of the board to programmatic participation in the work of the board. In effect, it does something worse than merely blur the distinction between the two constitutional parties in the life of the church. It creates an imbalance in the relationship between legislative and episcopal responsibilities. Moreover, it deprives the church of any real oversight of the programmatic work by legislative agencies.

Controversies surround several of the church's general boards and agencies. It is possible to have long debates over their programs and priorities.

But with the bishops of the church becoming policy-making participants in the work of the agencies, the church loses a resource for oversight of the agencies' activities. What's more, they risk losing the very credibility and moral authenticity that Bishop Mathews cited as their only real authority.

Sometimes, in occupying a presidential chair, a bishop is compelled to speak for the board. More properly, it seems, a bishop should speak to the board, offering oversight of its actions, advising the board about what it dare not overlook, and reaching a discerning as well as independent judgment on the directions of the agency.

By forsaking or at least diminishing their role in oversight, bishops may invite a perception that there are some things they might overlook. Perhaps, instead of having a bishop in the presidential chair when the governing board of an agency meets, the bishop or bishops in the room should remain on the side in order to oversee the board's work. From that angle, any bishop who is present could ask questions that keep a theological perspective and a missional focus upon the programs and policies of the board. Episcopal oversight in this form need not be adversarial, but it could—when necessary—be prophetic.

Ministry Not Territory

Oversight of the temporal and spiritual affairs of the church is the responsibility of United Methodist bishops. In that capacity, they are the "general" superintendents of the church. Their offices extend into the connection through what are called "district superintendents"—a strange title, actually, for it implies territoriality. In a church whose founder insisted that the world was his parish, the "district superintendency" sounds oddly parochial.

Of all the offices in Methodism, that of the district superintendent may be the most connectionally important and the least effectively resourced. Several studies over the years have noted that the superintendency is a hinge on which much of the connection moves. For most clergy and for the overwhelming majority of laity, the superintendent is the only judicatory leader in the denomination with whom they have any contact. She or he may be the only figure in the church, other than the pastor, who is accessible enough to answer questions about the programs and finances of the denomination.

In recent years, the role of the district superintendent has been diminishing.

For instance, with the growing congregationalization of the church, district superintendents have seemed less involved in or vital to local or regional ministries. Rarely will pastors or laity consult a superintendent about expanding evangelistic or social outreach into underserved neighborhoods. Rarely will superintendents feel motivated to develop missional strategies for a region. There is neither incentive nor reward for doing so.

In addition, many annual conferences have reduced the total number of superintendents and increased the workload of those that remain. In some, this has occurred because declines in the number of members and revenue dollars have forced budget cuts in the conference. Eliminating one superintendent's position looks like a quick way to save six figures in the bottom line of the budget. Other annual conferences have reorganized their staffing patterns and hired professionals with specialized responsibilities to handle program initiatives or personnel development. In some annual conferences, there is no way to finance such desirable ventures except by eliminating one or more superintendents' positions. Then the unused salaries can be diverted to fund the new positions for professional specialists.

But perhaps the most significant and lingering factor in diminishing the district superintendency has been most subtle. The change in title, away from "presiding elder," seems to have turned the nature of the office from that of a connectional minister to that of a middle manager who functioned as a regional or territorial bureaucrat.

It is true that other alterations in church polity have reduced the need for these positions to be mainly ministerial in character. Until a few decades ago, persons who were licensed to preach but were not ordained into the ministry lacked authorization to administer the sacraments. Therefore, about once every quarter, a district superintendent would conduct worship where only licensed preachers were appointed, would break the bread of life, and would sprinkle or pour the water of salvation. Now, however, every local pastor has sacramental authority in the place where she or he is appointed. The ministerial services of the superintendent are not needed—until a crisis occurs and some oversight is needed. But moral authority is hard to claim if one appears only in a time of crisis.

While some other Methodist bodies retained the title "presiding elder," United Methodists have found no need to reclaim it. Yet, if oversight and accountability are core issues for the recovery of Methodism, it could be valuable to reinstitute the ministry and reclaim the title.

Public Accountability and Oversight

One of the many places that could be identified as a landmark of John Wesley's failures is the church called Great St. Mary's in Oxford. As a fellow of Lincoln College in the university town, Wesley had some basic responsibilities to fulfill in return for the annual stipend he received. Tutoring students was one of them, of course. Another was preaching on some rotating schedule at one of the churches in the city.

On August 24, 1744, he had such an assignment for the feast of St. Bartholomew. He used the occasion to offer what became one of his better-known sermons, for that was the day he publicly challenged the spiritual depth and dedication of the community.[2]

Although that sermon is sometimes read as an appeal for individual Christians to be renewed with a more passionate personal faith, it allows other interpretations as well. A visit to Oxford and to St. Mary's several years ago helped me appreciate that one does not really understand a text unless one understands the context. When I stood in the nave of St. Mary's, I acquired a new respect for the context. The pulpit is elevated. Most of the people would have stood or sat on the flat floor of the nave, several feet below the level of the preacher. At the back of the nave was an elevated platform with special seating for the local dignitaries including the chancellor of the university and the city. The physical arrangement meant that, when he preached, Wesley would have been at eye level with the chancellor. So when he spoke about the inadequacies of an indifferent spirituality, he was probably not making eye contact so much with the citizenry in general as he was with the leadership of the city in particular.

His sermon that day was not an attempt at personal evangelism but a statement of public prophecy. Perhaps the best evidence that this was both the intent of his sermon and its effect is that he was never invited to preach at St. Mary's again. The public officials resented his message—which means they heard it loud and clear.

The recovery of Methodism will require a renewed sense of accountability for the oversight of the public arena. It will require a rediscovery of the capacity to render public witness. And it will be realized when Methodism, in its oversight of community beyond parish walls, declines its unwillingness to overlook what is evil or unjust, or is afraid to yearn for peace.

When anti-immigration fervor began to boil along the Texas-Mexico border recently, I heard about an incident that showed the church's courage to do just that. As the story was told to me, a health-care business establishment near the border was advised by its marketing consultant that it should take some steps to reach a more upscale clientele. The goal would be to have fewer patients and customers in mud-caked boots and sweat-stained work shirts, and more users in tasseled loafers and golf shirts.

Someone proposed a simple tactic that promised to have that result. Employees such as security and housekeeping personnel would be assigned new uniforms to wear on the job. Those who were stationed near the entrances would have their attire changed from a bland blue to a dark green. People who are familiar with the dark green uniform color know that it is the standard dress code for Border Patrol. Simply put, to outfit some of the staff in uniforms that made them resemble officers of the Border Patrol could create the impression that immigration checks were possible for anyone who entered the building. Moreover, it increased the possibility that actual Border Patrol agents would mingle with the staff and threaten passersby.

The tactic apparently worked. Within a very few days of the change in uniforms, the change in clientele was quite noticeable. The number of persons coming to the health-care facility who might be described as persons coming from the Mexican side of the border dropped substantially.

But some leaders in local churches observed it, too. Quietly, they approached the executives who managed the place and delivered a simple ultimatum—either switch the uniforms back to the nonthreatening color, or they would let the public know the cynical strategy that seemed to be driving their business. Not long after the message was sent and received, the uniforms were restored to a neutral color.

The recovery of Methodism requires Methodists to rediscover accountability for what happens in the public arena. In seeking the recovery of Methodism, there are some injustices we cannot overlook.

CHAPTER EIGHT

Forms of Recovery

"Let endurance have its full effect, so that you may be mature and complete."

(James 1:4)

The computer age has spawned a long line of jokes, according to engineering professor Henry Petroski. Many of them are roughly similar to this one. Three people are riding together in a car. One is a physicist, the second is an engineer, and the third is a computer scientist. Suddenly, they realize that there is a problem with the car. Smoke is pouring out of their vehicle. Then the engine stops.

Each of the three offers a comment on the situation. The physicist speaks first, suggesting that the difficulty with the car has to be worked out theoretically, for it is clearly a problem with torque. The engineer declares it to be a mechanical problem, which can be resolved with a technical adjustment. The computer scientist, however, takes a different approach. Instead of offering either a diagnosis of the difficulty or a potential solution to the problem, the computer scientist recommends that the three of them simply get out of the car, wait a minute, get back into the car, and restart it.[1]

In the computer age, that is what we do. While working on a document like a chapter in this book, one assumes that the act of touching letters on a keyboard will produce characters on the screen. But what happens if suddenly the cursor stops moving and letters quit appearing on the screen? What does one do if a dialogue box appears, reporting (as if the user did not know) that the program is not responding? What does one do if a thinly veiled threat appears on the screen, warning that any data that have not been saved until that point may be irretrievably lost? The user waits for a minute or so, and then hits Ctrl/Alt/Del, hoping that by rebooting the computer everything will be fine.

Why can't we just reboot Methodism? If it is not responding to the situation in the world, if it is not working effectively at the matters that we feel need spiritual or personal attention, if it seems to have locked up in such a way that we cannot access its resources, then perhaps we should just shut it down. Maybe, after waiting a while, someone can try to reboot it again!

Computers serve us splendidly. We truly could not function in the twenty-first century without them. At the same time, they have instilled in us some strange behavior patterns. We expect rapid, if not immediate, access to almost any piece of information that we want. We assume that communication with any person, anywhere in the world, at any time, should be possible. We trust that if, at any point, our systems are not operating, then all we have to do is wait for a fraction of a minute and restart. That may be the way most of us use computers. But that is not what I am trying to describe in proposing the recovery of Methodism.

My use of the word "recovery" is deliberately multivalent. First, I am using it in a medical sense, as a metaphor to take seriously the concern that Methodism is afflicted with poor health—physically, emotionally, and spiritually. Second, I am using it as a historical point of reference, trying metaphorically to think about the possibility that Methodism might rediscover its roots, reclaim its theological heritage, and rebuild by relearning what has been lost or neglected in the span of time. Third, I am using it in a visual sense, for I believe that Methodism need not be hamstrung by the harsh realities diagnosed about the movement in the present, that Methodism might not be burdened by bearing the unpleasant and unrighteous and unfaithful aspects of its past, and that instead Methodism might be beckoned by a vision of the future in which the movement will see itself transformed into all that God wills for a faithful people to become.

Recovery of Health

In one sense, by using the term "recovery" I want to take seriously what I have called the medicalization of Methodism. We have been living for decades with a sense that The United Methodist Church, possibly since its formation in 1968, has been in a serious state of declining health. Statistical losses of membership and attendance in United Methodism alone are enough to substantiate that point. More broadly, it appears that all of the theological and ecclesiastical traditions that trace their lineage to John Wesley feel weaker than they once did. At least it is true in North America—when the denominations that label themselves Methodist convene some discussions about common concerns, they sound like patients in a physician's waiting room comparing symptoms.

In United Methodism there is a pathological problem, perhaps a disease, whose symptoms include not only declining membership and declining worship attendance but also declining Sunday school attendance, a decaying infrastructure, deteriorating patterns of stewardship, and a deepening sense of depression about the institution. It has been said from time to time that congregations in the process of shrinking to a few members are entering a phase of institutional life akin to hospice care. Data about declines in the whole denomination can generate feelings of despair about the welfare of the church. One can conclude that, spiritually and emotionally and financially, Methodism is having a crisis of health.

If there has been a single day in my ministry when I faced most directly the sense that the church's health was at risk, it was an occasion during my district superintendency. A clergy member of the annual conference had been arrested, tried, and convicted of child abuse. He claimed that the charges were false and appealed the conviction. In the end, the state's criminal court system rejected his appeals and ordered him to begin serving his term of several years in a state prison. With no further appeal available to him, and with clear determination that he had been found guilty of a serious crime, I was assigned as one of the two superintendents to visit him in prison. It was not going to be a pastoral care session. It was to be an exercise in church discipline. We were there to explain that ecclesiastical charges would be filed against him on the basis of his having committed a crime and that he had two alternatives. He could insist upon his right to use all of United Methodism's judicial procedures and move toward a church trial. Or he could surrender his credentials and withdraw from the ordained ministry of the church.

The other superintendent and I took six hours to make the round-trip to the state prison. We spent about an hour with the felon who was our former colleague in ministry. Through that entire day we felt overwhelmed by great sadness and a sense of futility about the whole situation. Other than to conduct an exercise in church discipline, we were without any means to help the criminal recover from his loss of vocation, or to help his victims recover from the trauma of the abuse he had committed upon them, or to help his congregations recover from the knowledge that the denomination had entrusted him with the authority to engage in a ministry he had so completely dishonored.

Of course, this was one member of the clergy. And, to be sure, there have not been many ordained ministers convicted of criminal acts of violence toward persons or criminal acts of destruction toward property.

But we cannot take comfort in the false notion that offenses committed by leaders of the church have merely been the terrible acts of a few individuals. Some of the failures of the church have been systemic—not necessarily grievous, but grave nevertheless. And whether the recovery of Methodism can include recovering from unwise institutionalized problems and policies will determine if the church's health can be restored.

Among the data that are often cited to identify a crisis in the health of the church are statistics about the advancing average age of elders in the church. There is no point in trying to disagree with the numbers. But there is some value in trying to understand how those numbers became real.

First, when Methodists were recruiting candidates for the ordained ministry fifty years ago, the targeted group tended to be young men, many of whom were veterans of service in the military during World War II and the Korean War. They had opportunities to go to college on the GI Bill. They had options for enrolling in a growing number of Methodist theological seminaries. They had prospects for long careers in an expanding number of places for pastoral ministry. During the decades that followed, the emerging group of candidates for ordained ministry increasingly included women and men who had delayed pursuing a call to ministry, or who for reasons of gender discrimination had been deprived of the opportunity to pursue a call to ministry, or who had experienced a major change in spiritual or personal circumstances that led them to consider a call to ministry. The church has in effect added older cohorts or newly ordained ministers to the aging group of long-established ordained ministers. As a result, the average age has become older.

Second, during the same few decades, Methodism significantly reduced its support for and commitment to campus ministries at colleges and universities. Vastly larger numbers of persons have been seeking undergraduate degrees, yet denominational investments in providing specially trained clergy on campuses have waned considerably. Coupled with the fact that the denomination's institutions—camps, congregations, and confirmation classes—are less likely to produce larger numbers of potential candidates for ministry, many points of access to young adults have been lost. Most undergraduates tend to be young adults. So the weakening of campus ministry programs has deprived the church of a ready outreach to a whole generation. Strangely, some other denominations and independent religious groups have built very strong campus ministry programs. A number of them do not fully share—or, indeed, may be antithetical to—the theological heritage of Methodism. But they have found it possible to expand their efforts. Their work will fill a void left by the lack of a Methodist alternative.

Third, when Methodism has created some initiatives to reach youth and young adults, it has treated them tepidly. One of the truly successful ventures of The United Methodist Church in this regard has been a series of events, each of which was called "Exploration." These national gatherings drew upward of a thousand high school and college-age young people for spirited worship, interpersonal encounters, and vocational explorations about ministry as a career. Every time an "Exploration" event was scheduled it was filled to capacity. Yet the denomination decided that the events were so costly they could be held only once every four years. Somewhere in the systems of the denomination, somebody failed to count how much it would cost *not* to continue these initiatives.

Such system-wide failures have created problems from which Methodism will take a long time to recover. And before the recovery can begin, the problems must be noticed and the remedies for them must be supported. It is possible for a return to health on these matters if the diagnosis can be made and the treatment can begin soon.

There are other problems so deep-seated and so pervasive, however, that even mounting a major response may not be enough.

One of the terrible facts about Methodism's need for a recovery of health is that some sufferings leave wounds that never heal. Like some physical injuries that mend but never completely become well, like some emotional traumas that can be left behind but are never fully overcome, like some addictions to substances (such as drugs and alcohol) or to practices (such as gambling), one may be perpetually in pursuit of recovering but never in a full state of recovery. The harm may be too hard to remove. The hurt may run too deep.

Consider the damage that was done by centuries of gender discrimination in the lay and ordained ministries of the church. Limiting women to less than full participation in the life of the church deprived the denomination of countless gifts of leadership and service. Restricting the freedom of women to respond to a sense of call to ministry put them in restraints that left lasting scars on the church. As a result, women can always see with sharper eyes the sinister forces at work to prevent them from pursuing ordination into the ministry or election to the episcopacy—for such things are not fantasies, they are facts in the life of the church.

Consider the damage that was done by centuries of slavery, segregation, and racism in which Methodism was an active participant. Ending the Central Jurisdiction was a necessary step, creating the Commission on Religion and Race was a worthy act, and drafting nominating procedures to establish a permanent commitment to diversity were vital adjustments in the life of the church. Yet, no matter how many times a denomination sings "We Shall Overcome," it will not overcome completely the troubles that the church has caused for itself. Indeed, so grievous was the hurt that for some in Methodism—like the theologian and ordained minister in the African Methodist Episcopal Church, Dr. James Hal Cone—there is nothing that will ever take the anger away. Cone insists that he must continue to tell the truth about what white Christians inflicted on black people.

Yet there is an alternative to the justifiable anger that remains unrestrained rage. Dr. Cone insists that people hear the truth about the damage, destruction, and death the racist ways of the white church inflicted on black people. Archbishop Desmond Tutu insists on the same things, but he seeks a policy of truth and reconciliation.

The recovery of health is possible for the church in the world. To reach it, though, Methodism will have to be more brutally honest about the personal, the systemic, and the enduring problems an honest diagnosis will discover.

Recovery of Heritage

Methodism is a much more vast community of faith and history than any single denomination can embody. The United Methodist Church, for instance, is scarcely forty years old and has barely 10 percent of global Methodism's members. Any attempt to recover its heritage must explore far more terrain than simply its few institutional decades or limited expanse.

For example, one of the most dramatic statistical changes in Methodism occurred late in the nineteenth century, when there was a shift in the relationship between the number of persons who attended Methodist worship and the number of persons who were members of Methodist churches. In earlier days there were more attendees than members, but in later years members outnumbered attendees. Currently, on an average Sunday, the number of worshipers at United Methodist churches is less than 30 percent of the statistical membership.

In a curiously related matter, population data tend to show that nearly twice as many people in the United States claim to be Methodists as the denominational records can prove. If one were to add all of the membership statistics for all of the Methodist denominations beginning with United Methodists and moving through the rest, the total would still not come close to reaching the number of people who claim a Methodist affiliation. The point is simply that statistics are not necessarily reliable measurements of Methodism's vitality.

Of course, there is no guarantee that other measuring devices will detect a more vital church. For example, if some Methodists in the twenty-first century feel more at home with a Calvinist theological orientation—content with John Wesley's feeling that he was within a hair's breadth of Calvinism, despite his railing against it—then no effort to "recover" Wesleyan doctrine will seem to them sufficient if it lacks Reformed rigidity.

Recovering the heritage of Methodism actually involves some relatively simple tests. First there are the general rules against which any program or practice should be weighed. Methodists are generally enjoined to do no harm, to do good, and to attend to the ordinances of God—which include such matters as receiving the sacraments, studying the Scriptures, engaging in prayer, and loving our neighbors. Second, there are the general tenets of Methodist teaching—that holiness must be both personal and social, and that at the heart of the movement is the mission to reform the continent and spread scriptural holiness over the land. Third, there are the more specific emphases in the Methodist heritage on the primacy of God's gracious love, the willful participation in receiving God's grace, and the scripture way of salvation. On that last point, to recover its heritage Methodism must recover what it means to make sanctifying grace a lifelong journey. A dramatic conversion experience may be powerful and real. Repeated dramatic experiences of spiritual renewal at multiple moments in a lifetime may occur as well. Yet salvation is a process and not a point in time.

These are the basic emphases of Methodist belief and doctrine. It is certainly possible to insist on a denser definition of the theological heritage that Methodism must recover. Discussions of such matters are always welcome.

The problem is that Methodism has not found ways to have such conversations, at least not in the manner of a true dialogue where nuances matter, where subtleties surface, and where parties that disagree can engage in frank discussions of their disagreements. Methodists have seemed far more interested in sharpening the axes to attack their foes than putting the axes down and talking with their foes.

One reason is that the mechanisms Methodism seems to have available for such endeavors are so few. For example, John Wesley insisted that one of the means of grace was Christian conferencing. There is no doubt that Methodists have developed a polity built around numerous "conferences." It is, after all, at those conferences that we receive reports of the data showing our statistical declines in attendance, membership, and finances.

But, by another kind of assessment, something even more significant has been in a steady decline. Methodism has permitted the decline of Christian conferencing and has put in its place legislative conferencing. Anyone who has attended an annual conference or a General Conference has witnessed it. Someone drafts a statement or prepares a resolution or sends a petition to the conference. Parliamentary procedures are invoked to discuss, amend, or otherwise "perfect" the document. A vote is taken and the votes of the majority determine the destiny of the document.

Such things are the business of conferences in Methodism these days. But there is no assurance that any of it passes the test of Christian conferencing.

Take, for example, a resolution that someone submits about the topic of world peace. Assume that the writer of the resolution is an advocate for peace in the Middle East. Assume that a majority of the persons, who are present and eligible to vote, cast their ballots in favor of the resolution. The conference is now on record as supporting peace in the Middle East. However, if no Christian conferencing has occurred to discuss, debate, and determine the relationship between a majority for peace and a mission for peace, then the parliamentary vote is an empty act. Indeed, if the resolution has invoked the name of Jesus Christ as Prince of Peace but there is no missional commitment to be his disciples and work for peace, then at the very least a biblical commandment has been violated—for the resolution will have taken the Lord's name in vain.

Methodism has ample mechanisms for handling legislation. But it is possible that none of them is a means of grace. For legislative conferencing is not necessarily the same as Christian conferencing. Unless the process as well as the outcome clearly can be tied to the mission of the church, the means of grace were not used and grace may not have been conveyed at all. To recover the heritage of Methodism is to recover its gift for Christian conferencing.

Legislation is a blunt instrument. It cannot cut through hypocrisy. It cannot slice through deception. It cannot shave theological nuances. Legislation can only certify that a particular set of words secured a majority of the votes at a specific place and time on a single topic.

A case in point involves the actions of the General Conference of The United Methodist Church in 1992 regarding legislation on the ordained ministry. One of the church's seemingly ceaseless commissions to study the ministry presented a report to the conference, where a legislative committee basically took it apart and rebuilt it into a different document. During sessions of the legislative committee, various subgroups tried to craft some language that was sufficient to corral a majority of votes. At one point, someone returned from a lunch break with a paper napkin from a restaurant on which a definition of "ordination" had been written. Had anybody gone to a library to research the meaning of ordination in the history of the church? Had anyone consulted the broader church about definitions of ordination used in other bodies? Had anyone contacted a wide spectrum of theologians to engage in Christian conferencing about the significance of ordination? The answers, at least during the General Conference itself, were no, no, and no. For it was not necessary. In a legislative arena, one does not need wisdom or grace, just a majority.

Finally, the recovery of the heritage of Methodism requires a renewed awareness that the heritage is cumulative. That is, we cannot look back to the founding initiatives of Mr. Wesley and to the needs of the present without recognizing the importance of all that has accumulated in the intervening years. Similarly, we cannot accept the principle that an idea that seemed marvelously novel and creative at some point in the past qualifies as either good or bad for the present. It is blasphemous to declare some novelty to be a new word from the Lord—just because it is new. It is equally blasphemous to insist that some relic is a treasured word from the Lord—just because it is old. The only way to test whether we are recovering the heritage of Methodism is to experiment with it, to try it in a number of venues, and to chart the cumulative results. Can legislation to reestablish the office of class leader actually recover the power of the class meeting in Methodism? Or would it be better to test the concept of a class meeting again in some places where new congregations are being established, to engage in Christian conferencing about the results of the experiment, and then to offer the insights in a gracious but nonlegislative way to all of Methodism?

One of the reasons that Franklin Roosevelt was credited with being an outstanding leader was that during the Great Depression he showed a willingness to experiment with new ideas, to try new programs, and to let some novel theories be tested in small practice. Sometimes, it takes many experiments and many practices to discern whether something will actually work.

Engineers at NASA carry in the folklore of their agency a story that dates back to the earliest days of the space program, when the original *Mercury* astronauts were first being launched into orbit. A problem had been discovered in the fuel line of the rocket. Because of the extremely cold temperatures associated with certain liquid fuels, NASA continued to have problems with condensation, which was drawing water into the fuel system. A means had to be found to draw or disperse the water away from that area. As they worked on the problem through a series of experiments, they met failure after failure. They identified the goal as water dispersion and assigned to each experiment a number. The number of failed efforts grew. After they realized that water dispersion test number thirty-nine was not going to succeed, they began water dispersion test forty. That one actually worked. They used the chemical to solve the problem. And not long afterward, the chemical they created was marketed in a blue can bearing the initials of the code name "water dispersion forty"—WD-40.

The recovery of the heritage of Methodism is an effort to find again the facets of the faith that get lost or left behind when it is conceived as a narrow set of convictions, worship practices, or political positions. To recover Methodism is to realize that no single ideological direction or practical discipline can capture everything that is true about the movement.

Yet there are a few things that, if absent from the Methodism we recover, will belie any claim to being Methodist at all. To recover Methodism's heritage is to require both social holiness and personal holiness—not a personal holiness that eventually leads to social holiness, nor a commitment to social justice that calls upon a prayerful personal holiness, but the simultaneous presence of both. Only if it is about the transformation of individuals *and* the transformation of the world is it Methodist. Only if it is about the process of salvation pointing toward a goal of perfect love is it Methodist.

Recovery of Hope

This means that the "recovery" of Methodism must involve an orientation to and a vision of the future. This is not a theoretical notion. It is a practical approach to shaping the institutions of the church. Bishop James K. Mathews, for instance, says of the episcopacy in Methodism that it is not "an *historic episcopate*" but "a *futuric episcopate*." He takes that to mean the episcopacy "becomes what the people, under God's guidance and in response to the demands of history, determine it shall be."[2] The recovery of Methodism, to put it another way, is an eschatological exercise in discerning what God is beckoning and equipping the church to become.

To do that, we must be wary of the distractions that may momentarily lure us with glitter, or tease us with novelty, or please us with ephemeral joy, when it is only eternal joy that can bring peace. We also must be wary of the distractions that deny the existence of any serious problems, the counterfeit ideas that may distract us toward false or fruitless proposals for addressing problems, and the material distractions that might make us lose our vision for the mission of the church.

We need to recover our focus. And our focus must never be on making the church bigger but on reaching the world better. It must never be on settling into congregations but on setting congregations in the context of a global community. It must never be on worrying about whether Methodism casts a smaller shadow on the landscape but whether it shines a brighter light for the spiritual journey.

In the cemetery that fills most of the churchyard surrounding the parish church at Epworth lies the burial site of a man named Thomas Cutforth. A convicted thief who was hanged in the Market Square of Epworth for his crime, Cutforth was not part of the Epworth parish nor was he an individual in the care of the rector. By the custom of the era, the man's body was to be left on display as a public notice of what criminals might face. But the rector, Samuel Wesley, was drawn by a vision of grace that surpassed his respect for judgment. He personally walked to Market Square, cut the rope, took the body down from the gallows, and carried it to the churchyard where he conducted a simple funeral on March 27, 1720.

His son John Wesley, who was sixteen years old at the time, experienced many forms of grace in his own spiritual journey. The knowledge that his father had performed such an act of pure grace toward one who merited nothing gave some sharper focus to his vision of just how practical the works of grace could be.

As a first step, the recovery of hope means seeing beyond the boundaries of any parish or congregation and casting a vision that is as broad as the world. Methodism is already a global presence. Its organized churches and denominations span the earth. What is needed now is to be sure that every local church understands its context as not just parochial, not just regional, not just national, but always global. The church has to grasp what its people already experience in their personal and professional lives. Through e-mail and webcam communications, individuals cross international boundaries and time zones. In secular business and commercial enterprises, anyone who earns a living is involved in the global economy.

When my wife and I traveled to Asia, the trip from Dallas to Malaysia involved a number of stops—in Chicago, in Shanghai, and in Kuala Lumpur. In that last leg, a six-hour flight from Shanghai to Kuala Lumpur, she happened to be in the middle seat of our row, next to a young woman. The two of them tried to initiate a conversation. Finding a language in common proved to be a challenge. The young woman spoke a little English and tried to talk with my wife, who speaks only English. But the limited vocabulary and ambient noise from the aircraft's jet engines made understanding difficult.

Yet it was a long flight, and after a while they developed a way to communicate. The young woman pulled a text-messaging device from her purse and typed questions or thoughts in English on the screen. My wife read them and replied orally. Back and forth they went, for hours. What we learned about our companion was that she was traveling from China to Malaysia for a few days of vacation, and that her home was actually in Beijing. However, she was working in Tokyo for a Japanese company. The next set of exchanges went roughly like this.

"What does your company in Tokyo do?"

"The company owns several Kentucky Fried Chicken restaurants."

"And your job?"

"I work with the vendors who provide vegetables to our restaurants. Mostly I buy from vendors in California in the U.S."

It was an amazing conversation. Across the boundaries of multiple language differences, we learned that we were seated with a woman who was her own example of the global economy—a Chinese woman, employed in Japan, working for a company based in the United States, purchasing produce from farms in the western states where the vegetables were probably harvested by Latin American laborers.

Later, in Singapore, that vision was more deeply reinforced. We worshiped on Sunday morning in a Methodist congregation whose building sits in an Indian neighborhood. During the service, we learned about the local church's missionary outreach, specifically to Thailand, where they have established four new congregations. The report on these missionary efforts was offered by the chair of the mission program, who happened to be an engineer from Wales.

The recovery of Methodism requires surrendering any pretense that the movement can thrive within parochial or national boundaries. The world really is our parish now, and that must be the horizon to which we extend our vision.

But that is only one step. The second is that our vision must extend well beyond our own time. Back in the 1940s, a Methodist minister named Paul Martin talked with one of his church members, Joe Perkins, about something that only a person of significant wealth would ever be likely to hear from a pastor. The message was simply that God had blessed Mr. Perkins with the capacity to acquire more earthly resources than he could properly limit in his giving to their local church. But he could have an impact on forming leaders of Methodism until the end if he were to provide an endowment to a university for its theological school. It was an act of vision for Paul Martin to see beyond his, and his parishioner's, own time.

Several years later, in the early 1950s, after the endowment had been transmitted, the dean of the theological school and the president of the university determined that they needed to end the university's policy of racial segregation. The private university, owned by the church, could not be limited to white students only. When the first black students were admitted, all five of them were enrolled in the school of theology. When one of the five arranged with a white classmate to room together for the next academic year, some of the university's trustees—including Mr. Perkins—wondered if this would end the experiment in integrating the university. At that point his wife, Lois, with a vision that extended beyond her own time and beyond the fears of segregationists in Dallas, told her husband that the racial barriers had to end.

The recovery of hope in Methodism involves the courage to have a vision beyond the boundaries of our present time. Biblical faith—

and therefore Methodist faith—is the substance of things hoped for, and the evidence of things not seen. With courage enough to see that far, we will be touching a mystery incapable of being captured by statistical evidence. We can gain access to it only by the means of grace such as prayer and the sacraments of faith. It may frustrate many Methodists who would prefer more method and less mystery in the effort. Yet it is the gift of grace.

In one of the great pieces of Methodist doctrine, Charles Wesley answered a question about Methodism's teaching regarding the Eucharist. Do Methodists believe in transubstantiation? Do Methodists believe in the real presence of Christ at the sacrament? Do Methodists simply believe the elements at the Table are a memorial of Christ's last supper with the disciples?

He answered the questions by putting a frame around another question.

> Let the wisest mortals show how we the grace receive;
> feeble elements bestow a power not theirs to give.
> Who explains the wondrous way, how through these the virtue came?
> These the virtue did convey, yet still remain the same.
>
> Sure and real is the grace, the manner be unknown;
> only meet us in thy ways and perfect us in one.
> Let us taste the heavenly powers, Lord, we ask for nothing more.
> Thine to bless, 'tis only ours to wonder and adore.[3]

The recovery of Methodism will be a recovery of grace and mystery.

NOTES

Preface

1. *Wall Street Journal*, April 3, 2007, B1.
2. See Judicial Council Decision No. 243, November 10, 1966.
3. Dan Dick, in an unpublished internal research update produced for the General Board of Discipleship of The United Methodist Church, drew these data from the United States Census and from the *Handbook of Denominations in the United States*, published by the *National Council of Churches*.

Introduction

1. Henry Petroski, *Success Through Failure: The Paradox of Design* (Princeton: Princeton University Press, 2006), 169.

Chapter 1: Checking the Vital Signs

1. "The Baptismal Covenant III," in *The United Methodist Hymnal: Book of United Methodist Worship* (Nashville: The United Methodist Publishing House, 1989), 45.
2. Petroski, *Success Through Failure*, 59–60.
3. David Van Biema, "Mother Teresa's Crisis of Faith," *Time*, August 23, 2007.
4. "A Service of Word and Table II," *The United Methodist Hymnal: Book of United Methodist Worship* (Nashville: The United Methodist Publishing House, 1989), 12.
5. *Dallas Morning News*, March 27, 2007, 7A.

Chapter 2: When the Positive Is Negative and the Negative Is Positive

1. Charles Wesley, "And Are We Yet Alive?" in *The United Methodist Hymnal: Book of United Methodist Worship* (Nashville: The United Methodist Publishing House, 1989), 553, stanza 3.

Chapter 3: Methodism Under a Microscope

1. Other United Methodists have similarly been elected to public office. Emmanuel Cleaver of Missouri, for example, has served as mayor of Kansas City and as a member of the House of Representatives from the fifth congressional district.

2. Sockman actually began his ministry at Madison Avenue Methodist Episcopal Church in New York. It merged with the East Sixty-first Street Methodist Episcopal Church during the first decade of his ministry, and the newly formed congregation took the name Christ Church, Methodist.

3. Justo L. González, "Hispanic United Methodists and American Culture," in *The People(s) Called Methodists: Forms and Reforms of Their Life*, ed. William B. Lawrence, Dennis M. Campbell, Russell E. Richey (Nashville: Abingdon, 1998), 249.

4. Ernest T. Campbell, "A Lover's Quarrel with Preaching," in *What's the Matter with Preaching Today?* ed. Mike Graves (Louisville: Westminster John Knox Press, 2004), 57.

5. At that time, prior to the changes in the orders of ministry in 1996, only elders were authorized to wear stoles.

Chapter 4: A Fear of Fractures

1. Sarah Kreutziger, "Is There a New Role for Lay Leadership," in *Questions for the Twenty-first Century Church*, ed. Russell E. Richey, William B. Lawrence, Dennis M. Campbell (Nashville: Abingdon, 1999), 120.

Chapter 5: Finding a Mission

1. Michael Kazin, *A Godly Hero: The Life of William Jennings Bryan* (New York: Knopf, 2006), 174.

2. Harold Fredric, *The Damnation of Theron Ware* (Cambridge, Mass.: Belknap Press, Harvard University, 1960).

3. James Russell Lowell, "Once to Every Man and Nation," in *The Methodist Hymnal* (Nashville: The Methodist Publishing House, 1964), 242.

4. Wesley claimed that he could preach to as many as twenty thousand in Gwennap Pit at one time. When our tour group gathered there, I mentioned that statistic. There were many skeptics, until one engineer in the group confessed that he had done some quick mathematical calculations and determined that, indeed, such a number was quite possible.

Chapter 6: American Methodism and Methodism of Americans

1. Gerald Kennedy, *The Methodist Way of Life* (Englewood Cliffs, N.J.: Prentice Hall, 1958).

2. F. Gerald Ensley, "American Methodism: An Experiment in Secular Christianity," vol. 3, *The History of American Methodism*, general ed. Emory Stevens Bucke (Nashville: Abingdon, 1964), 615–27.

3. Kazin, *A Godly Hero*, 174, 267.

4. Bill Coles, "A Speech That Made Abolition History," in *Wall Street Journal*, May 12, 2007, P14.

5. Joseph T. Reiff, "What Became of the 28?" a paper presented to the Wesley Studies Group at the American Academy of Religion, November 2006.

Chapter 7: Oversight and Accountability

1. James K. Mathews and William B. Oden, eds., *Vision and Supervision: A Sourcebook of Significant Documents of the Council of Bishops of The United Methodist Church, 1968–2002* (Nashville: Abingdon, 2003), 607.

2. Richard P. Heitzenrater, *Wesley and the People Called Methodists* (Nashville: Abingdon, 1995), 150.

Chapter 8: Forms of Recovery

1. Petroski, *Success Through Failure*, 58.

2. James K. Mathews, *Set Apart to Serve: The Meaning and Role of the Episcopacy in the Wesleyan Tradition* (Nashville: Abingdon, 1985), 264.

3. Charles Wesley, "O the Depth of Love Divine," *The United Methodist Hymnal: Book of United Methodist Worship* (Nashville: The United Methodist Publishing House, 1989), 627.